THIS USED TO BE ST. LOUIS

NINI HARRIS

Reedy Press
PO Box 5131
St. Louis, MO 63139
www.reedypress.com

Library of Congress Control Number: 2017934686

ISBN: 9781681061139

Front cover: *Carondelet Historical Society (top), Missouri History Museum Library and Archives (bottom)* Back cover: *Carondelet Historical Society (left), Private Collection (middle), Don Korte (right)*

Printed in the United States of America
19 20 21 22 23   5 4 3 2

CONTENTS

INTRODUCTION

St. Louis history is revealed in the bricks and mortar of its buildings, in the pavement of its streets, and in the landscapes of its parks.

During its history, St. Louis played critical roles as the gateway to the American West, in the Union victory in the Civil War, in industrializing the American economy, and in mobilizing to defeat the Nazis in World War II.

While St. Louis served as the stage for these great sagas of American history, the city was also absorbing waves of new citizens from around the world, each bringing their own cultures and traditions.

These cultures differed radically. French colonial culture allowed slavery while accepting marriage between Europeans and Native Americans. African Americans lived and worked and some prospered as free men in St. Louis while Missouri was still a slave state. German immigrants fought for abolition, defended the Union, and later helped create outstanding public schools. Impoverished Irish, who had been denied education by their English rulers, achieved middle-class status in two generations in St. Louis. Early Jewish settlers were integrated among the Germans. Later, Orthodox Jews from Poland and Russia formed enclaves on the near north side, where they faced hardship but also enjoyed the freedom to succeed. Waves of immigrants from Hungary, Italy, China, Croatia, Serbia, Lebanon, Poland, and Bohemia built distinctive communities that enriched St. Louis. And in the early twentieth century, a great migration from the South brought more whites and African Americans from rural backgrounds.

The story of each old factory, each nineteenth-century brick cottage, and each corner storefront takes twists and turns through these layers of St. Louis history. Each reflects some facet of ethnic history, neighborhood life a century ago, the city's entrepreneurial spirit, its exceptional architectural heritage, or its citizens' patriotism.

The stories of what these individual sites used to be are the puzzle pieces that compose the rich texture of St. Louis history.

1

Gateway Arch National Park

The spectacular grounds of Gateway Arch National Park—providing a dramatic setting for one of the modern wonders of the world, the 630-foot-tall stainless steel Gateway Arch—have gone through a series of incarnations. French and Creole settlers turned the wilderness riverbanks into a frontier outpost. Eventually that outpost evolved into a grid of streets lined with beautifully crafted Victorian-era warehouses. More than five hundred buildings lined the streets that crisscrossed the area. The manufactured goods needed on the frontier—traps, pots, cutlery, pans, fabric, rope, canvas, pottery, glass, and hardware—passed through these warehouses on their way to the American West.

The levee, which fed those warehouses, was the busiest place in town, with boats stacked on the riverfront often two and three deep. The drays came and went in an endless stream. The freight from steamers—in barrels, crates, and bales—was piled high as houses.

The critical role the St. Louis riverfront played in not only local commerce, but in American commerce, ended when the Eads Bridge and its railroad tunnel carried business over and away from the riverfront. The historic riverfront began a steady decline. By the 1890s, instead of being the heart of the city's commerce, much of the riverfront was underused and slowly being forgotten.

THIS USED TO BE: A Forgotten Warehouse District

NOW IT'S: Gateway Arch National Park

LOCATION: Downtown St. Louis Riverfront

The declining St. Louis riverfront at the turn of the century. The railroad tracks carried commerce over and away from the historic levee. (Postcard from a private collection)

Author Theodore Dreiser described a scene on one corner of the riverfront district in the early 1890s when he worked at the *St. Louis Republic* newspaper. The newspaper offices were located at 3rd and Chestnut Streets, currently on the grounds of Gateway Arch National Park, directly east of the Hyatt Regency hotel.

"The *Republic* was in a tumbledown old building in a fairly deserted neighborhood in that region near the waterfront from which the city proper had been steadily growing away for years," Dreiser wrote.

"The office was so old and rattletrap. . . . The elevator was a slow and wheezy box, bumping and creaking and suggesting immediate collapse. The boards of the entrance-hall and city editorial room squeaked under one's feet."

Dreiser continued: "The windows facing east looked out upon a business court or alley where trucks and vans creaked all day but which at night was silent as the grave, as was this entire wholesale neighborhood. The buildings directly opposite were decayed wholesale houses of some unimportant kind where in slimsy rags of dresses or messy trousers and shirts girls and boys of from fourteen to twenty worked all day. . . ."

2

MetroLink Tunnel

MetroLink trains enter an arched tunnel of giant, rough-cut stones that passes underneath downtown St. Louis. Each day, two hundred MetroLink trains carrying tens of thousands of passengers on their way to jobs, schools, or baseball games travel through this 4,095-foot tunnel. The tunnel, which feels like ancient catacombs, connects the Eads Bridge with the Busch Stadium station.

The tunnel and its route resulted from efforts to stop James B. Eads from bridging the Mississippi River. Opponents of the bridge, including Chicago interests, forced it to connect with St. Louis on the north side of downtown at Washington Avenue, far from the St. Louis railbeds. Another challenge was posed by Congress, which required that the bridge be so high above the water that it would carry the rails above the levee and onto Washington Avenue in the heart of downtown.

The prospect that every day scores of freight trains would be cutting through the streets of downtown's business district as they spewed smoke and sparks was unacceptable.

Self-taught engineer James B. Eads proposed the tunnel as the way to connect the railroad bridge (on the northern edge of downtown) with the railbeds in Mill Creek (on the southern edge of downtown) without permanently disrupting downtown street traffic. The tunnel would follow Washington Avenue west to about 7th Street, then turn south.

The tunnel was constructed as an open cut. Its sides were so near the building lines that the foundations of downtown's warehouses and office buildings had to be shored during construction. After its walls were built, the roof of the tunnel and the street surfaces were rebuilt. The tunnel was constructed as a double tunnel, with a partition wall separating the sets of tracks.

Each side of the double tunnel was fourteen feet wide, except at the curve where they were fifteen feet wide. At the top of the arch, each side was sixteen feet six inches tall.

The deck of the new Eads Bridge connected with Washington Avenue, and the lower rail deck directed the trains into a tunnel under the streets of downtown St. Louis. (Illustration courtesy of Carondelet Historical Society)

THIS USED TO BE: Railroad Tunnel for the Eads Bridge

NOW IT'S: MetroLink Tunnel

LOCATION: Downtown St. Louis

3

Mill Creek Pumping Station

At the foot of Chouteau Avenue, just south of downtown, railroad tracks parallel the giant floodwall. Brilliant graffiti covers the concrete wall, which has been designated as a legal place for ever-changing graffiti murals. The four-story orange-brick Mill Creek Pumping Station abuts the wall, only feet south of Chouteau. Built in 1970, this station is a key to understanding the early village of St. Louis: It marks the site where the old Mill Creek, now a sewer line, once flowed into the Mississippi; it marks the early southern boundary of St. Louis; and it marks the site of an Indian village adjacent to St. Louis in the 1760s.

A postcard of scenic Chouteau's Pond, which stretched westward from present-day Busch Stadium to beyond present-day Union Station. The booming growth in population and industry during the early nineteenth century polluted the pond and turned it into a health hazard. It was drained after the cholera epidemic of 1849. (Postcard from a private collection)

The original name of Mill Creek was "Petite Riviere," or the little river, which formed the southern edge of colonial-era St. Louis. By 1767,

THIS USED TO BE: A Peoria Indian Village

NOW IT'S: Mill Creek Pumping Station

LOCATION: Downtown St. Louis

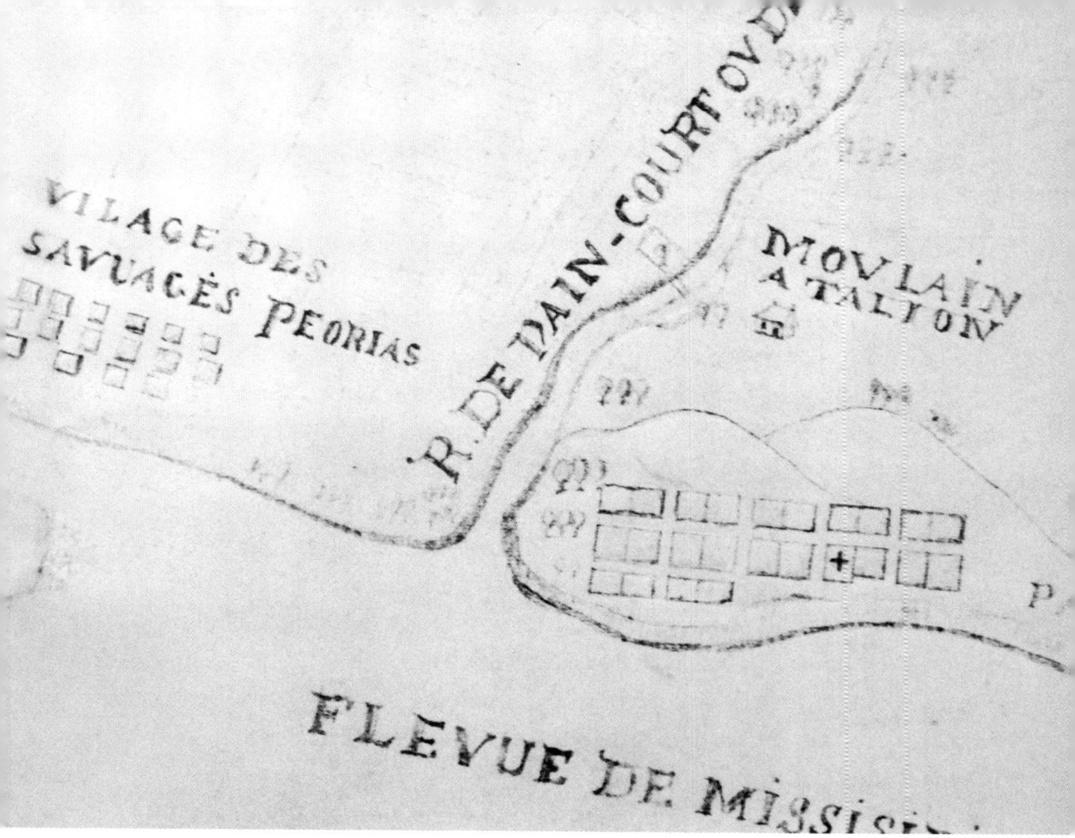

The southern edge of downtown St. Louis, around Chouteau Avenue, as shown on the map of St. Louis by Guy Dufossat. This copy of the map was traced by Norbury Wayman in 1953. (Collections of the St. Louis Public Library)

Joseph Taillon had dammed the creek or little river to power a mill at what is now 8th and Spruce Streets, near the Busch Stadium MetroLink station. That dam, later bought by Auguste Chouteau, created a long, wandering body of water named Chouteau's Pond.

A map executed by French military engineer Guy Dufossat and dated October 1767 shows the little river flowing into the Mississippi. On the map, Dufossat identified St. Louis by its nickname, Pain Court, or short of bread, referring to the wheat shortage in the fur trading post.

Curiously, his map also shows a small village on the banks of the Mississippi that would have been adjacent to the south side of the pumping station. Where there are now railroad tracks and the floodwall, his map also showed "Vilage des Savuages Peorias," or village of the Peoria Indians.

4

Streets of Laclede's Landing

Though twenty-first-century employees of engineering, public relations, and law firms along with apartment residents come and go from the historic buildings of Laclede's Landing, the streets of the Landing still echo the raw energy of the mid-nineteenth century. Then, draft horses pulled wagonloads of manufactured goods from the riverboats over red granite cobblestones to the warehouses lining the streets. The Landing's nineteenth-century warehouses were built of brick, limestone quarried along the river, and cast iron smelted in mills near the river. Huge wood piers and joists from ancient cypress trees timbered in Missouri swamps support the floors in these warehouses, which still recall the days when the St. Louis riverfront was feeding and supplying the American West.

The streets, however, had an even earlier life, when Frenchmen, Creoles, Indian and African slaves, and free blacks walked them. They are part of the very grid of mud pathways of colonial-era St. Louis that Pierre Laclede and Auguste Chouteau surveyed. The pathways framed the nine blocks at the north end of the French fur trading post. These rectangular blocks measured 240 feet wide, facing the river, and 300 feet deep. Laclede halved or quartered these blocks, assigning sections to early settlers. They built small houses, many only one room, of poteau-en-terre construction with the logs planted upright in trenches (instead of Anglo-style horizontal log construction). At first they thatched the roofs, but later they roofed the houses with wood shingles. Their small houses, which also served as their workshops or businesses, measured about twenty feet square.

The aroma of cinnamon still permeates the third floor of the Old Judge Building at 710 North 2nd Street, from when the nineteenth-century building was used as a spice warehouse.

The red and gray granite cobblestones paving the streets of Laclede's Landing. (Photo by Dylan Weber Callahan)

In 1804, when St. Louis was transferred to the United States, sixteen structures, including two horse-powered mills, were scattered along the streets of Laclede's Landing.

THIS USED TO BE: Mud Pathways of Colonial St. Louis

NOW IT'S: Streets of Laclede's Landing

LOCATION: Downtown St. Louis

5

Raeder Place

The seven-story Raeder Place building on Laclede's Landing, occupied by high-tech firms and the ever-popular Old Spaghetti Factory, was once the scene of "brakes," or daily auctions of leaf tobacco. Both foreign and domestic buyers attended the auctions in the elegant tobacco warehouse, which was completed in 1874 and clad with an elaborate cast-iron facade (the finest remaining cast-iron facade in the state). Historic Raeder Place, however, is the third generation of significant buildings constructed on this riverfront property.

During the colonial era, the site was tied to French fur-trading families. Trader Jacques Clamorgan owned the land and built a small home on the property. Later, he sold the parcel to Pierre Chouteau, son of St. Louis founder Auguste Chouteau and owner of the Missouri Fur Company.

During Missouri's territorial days, Irishman Thomas Brady bought the property and began building the Missouri Hotel in 1819. The new two-story stone hotel dwarfed many of the old French buildings then on the riverfront. Thick wood shingles roofed the hotel. Chimneys and dormer windows punctuated its gabled roof. Soon the substantial building was the premier hotel of the Mississippi Valley. The comparatively spacious hotel could accommodate the fourteen senators and forty-three representatives gathered there for the first Missouri territorial legislature. It convened in the hotel in September 1820, the year before Missouri was admitted to the Union.

By the time of the post–Civil War building boom, the hotel was dwarfed by the next generation of buildings—the massive brick and cast-iron warehouses. German immigrant Christian Peper razed the by then antiquated hotel and commissioned another German immigrant, prolific architect Frederick Raeder, to design a tobacco warehouse for the prime riverfront property. Over a century later, when the warehouse was renovated for multi-tenant use as part of the reincarnated Laclede's Landing, it was renamed Raeder Place in honor of its architect.

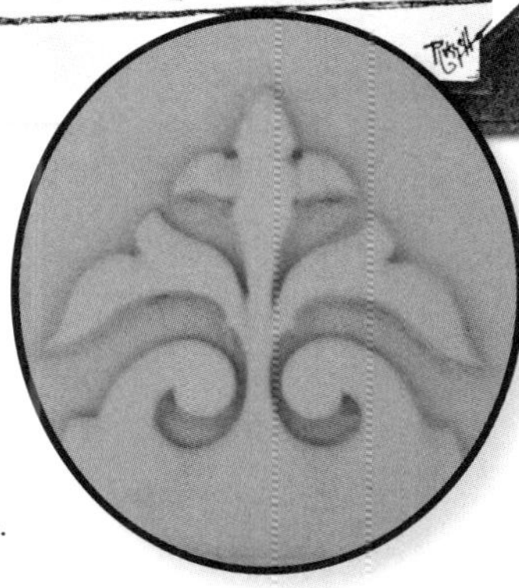

Missouri's first governor, Alexander McNair, was inaugurated in the Missouri Hotel, and two generals who would become American presidents were guests there—General William Henry Harrison and General Zachary Taylor. (Drawing courtesy of the Missouri Historical Society)

Cast-iron detail on a column of Raeder Place. (Photograph by NiNi Harris)

THIS USED TO BE: The Site of the Territorial Legislature

NOW IT'S: Raeder Place

LOCATION: 719–727 North 1st Street (at Morgan)

6 William A. Kerr Foundation

The dignified, beige brick and stone William A. Kerr Foundation building, originally a bathhouse and spa, is tucked into the corner of O'Fallon and Lewis Streets on the north riverfront. It sits between the huge hulks of century-old warehouses, early twentieth-century power plant buildings, railroad tracks, the trailhead of the North Riverfront Trail, and the banks of the Mississippi.

While the surrounding buildings speak of hundred-year-old technology, the William A. Kerr Foundation building has been renovated to showcase sustainable and green building practices suitable for twenty-first-century homes and small businesses. The renovation of the nineteenth-century bathhouse reflects the mission of the foundation to help groups committed to enriching the environment and promoting health and accessibility.

The bathhouse building, facing O'Fallon, sat atop a well that was drilled between 1849 and 1854. The well reached to a depth of almost 2,200 feet, offering water rich in sulphur and minerals thought to be medicinal. Its fountain attracted a steady crowd. In 1894, the classical-style bathhouse was built over the well. It cost $14,000 to build and featured Roman arches, blind arches, small oculus windows, and a low hipped roof.

The well was originally drilled to obtain pure water for the Belcher Sugar Refining Company, which occupied much of the north riverfront district during the mid-nineteenth century. The well water, however, was not suitable for refining sugar.

The formal entrance to the riverfront spa that has been transformed into the headquarters for the William A Kerr Foundation. (Photo by NiNi Harris)

When the water was piped to a new Belcher Bath and Hotel in downtown St. Louis, the classical-style bathhouse on the riverfront was closed. The riverfront bathhouse building was converted into a warehouse, and a small addition with loading docks was added in 1919. The building served as a warehouse until its renovation as the home of the William A. Kerr Foundation.

THIS USED TO BE: Belcher Bathhouse

NOW IT'S: William A. Kerr Foundation

LOCATION: 21 O'Fallon Street

7 Hilton at the Ballpark

The Hilton at the Ballpark—with its pair of towers rising within a hundred yards of Busch Stadium—is a landmark to both local and out-of-town baseball fans. Catty-corner from the Old Courthouse, the hotel's rooftop bar and restaurant offer breathtaking views of the region. The walls of windows on the towers give every room views of downtown, including some views that look right into Busch Stadium. The towers rise from a pavilion that covers two city blocks.

That pavilion, which has been expanded and altered, was built as the Spanish Pavilion for the New York World's Fair of 1964–65. The *New York Times*'s art critic declared the pavilion, designed by Javier Carvajal, "the best total work of art" at the fair.[1] It won the gold medal as the fair's "Most Outstanding Building."

When St. Louis businessman Harold Koplar visited the fair, he was bowled over the by the building and thought it should be in St. Louis. He encouraged then mayor Alfonso Cervantes to see it, and the two men flew to New York to tour the pavilion.

Cervantes later wrote, "Even the smell was fascinating: the 350,000 Flemish pine blocks that made up the Moorish ceiling gave off a rich, exotic aroma."[2]

Though the Spanish government was willing to present the building to a group who would put it to good use, the recipient had to pay to dismantle and move the pavilion. A new civic group, the St. Louis Ambassadors, raised the $800,000 that had to be guaranteed for moving costs.

With plenty of hoopla, the Spanish Pavilion—offering gallery space and a 780-seat theater—opened in downtown St. Louis as an international center.

It went bankrupt.

In 1976, the Spanish Pavilion was put back in use with the construction of a hotel tower that rose from the pavilion's courtyard. The pavilion was converted into the lobby, restaurants, and meeting rooms of the new hotel. The second hotel tower was added in 1981.

A postcard showing the Spanish Pavilion ca. 1970 from tulip-filled Kiener Plaza. (Postcard from a private collection)

THIS USED TO BE: Spanish Pavilion at the New York World's Fair

NOW IT'S: Hilton at the Ballpark

LOCATION: 1 South Broadway

8 ··

Spire Energy Headquarters

A gleaming jumble of giant, black-glass geometric blocks forms the Spire Energy Building at 700 Market Street. Built in 1977 and designed by the architect who championed the postmodern style, Phillip Johnson, the office building sparkles at night like a monumental sculptural backdrop for Kiener Plaza and City Garden. A thirty-one-story, black-glass tower built in 1981 fills the adjacent block at 800 Market Street.

Together, these glass-sheathed, late-twentieth-century office buildings cover the two-block site of Hop Alley, where St. Louis's Chinese community conducted businesses, lived, and played fan-tan on Sundays.

Hop Alley, St. Louis's Chinatown, revolved around 8th Street between Market and Walnut. Though the origins of the Chinese community date to the arrival of Chinese railroad workers from San Francisco in 1869, references to Hop Alley first appear in the early 1890s. By that time, Chinese hand laundries operated throughout the city.

On Sundays, Chinese Americans closed their laundries and took streetcars to Market and 8th Streets. Here were Chinese groceries offering teas, cigars, cooking ingredients, and embroidered cloth. Stores supplied Chinese laundries, restaurants, and chop suey shops. The Chinese proprietors, who usually lived behind their businesses, decorated Hop Alley with dragons and lanterns for the Chinese New Year.

Federal restrictions on emigration from China kept the Chinese community small; it numbered only a few hundred. With the post–World War II generation moving to the suburbs, Hop Alley dwindled to about thirty elderly men in the laundry trade. Civic leaders corralled the parcels in the disappearing alley and nearby neglected blocks for Busch Stadium II and the surrounding improvements and redevelopment.

The 1888 city directory lists seventy-six Chinese laundries.

Photo of Hop Alley in 1910. (Courtesy of the Missouri Historical Society)

THIS USED TO BE: Hop Alley, St. Louis's Chinatown

NOW IT'S: Spire Energy Headquarters

LOCATION: 700 Market Street

9 Walnut Street at 7th Street

For a decade, the two-story, gray, cast-concrete building that stands across the street from Ballpark Village was an after-the-game destination for baseball fans. From 2006 to 2016, this mid-century modern building housed the steak and seafood restaurant operated by Cardinals player and announcer Mike Shannon. When burlesque was in its prime, the three-story Standard Theater, with its gaudy Gilded Age facade, stood on this site, facing Walnut.

The theater offered ribald productions, and was connected to unusual local and national figures. The city's Irish political boss, Edward Butler, built the theater with seating for more than twenty-four hundred patrons in 1883. Butler, known for his princely manners, reportedly controlled and taxed all the vice in St. Louis. His theater was called "a vulgar burlesque theater" by revolutionary American author Theodore Dreiser, who was then the drama critic for the *Globe-Democrat*. Dreiser reported that the Standard's ticket taker was Frank James, brother and partner of the "amazing Jesse who terrorized Missouri and the Southwest as an outlaw at one time and enriched endless dime novel publishers afterward."[3]

Frank James had also worked at the racetrack at the fairground, now Fairground Park at Grand Boulevard and Natural Bridge Avenue in North City.

In the early 1890s, "There were seven or eight theaters in St. Louis, three or four of them staging only that better sort of play known as a first-class attraction; the others giving melodrama, vaudeville and burlesque," according to then *Globe-Democrat* theater critic Theodore Dreiser.[4]

A portrait of the notorious Frank James (1843–1915), who worked as the ticket taker at a burlesque theater in downtown St. Louis. (Courtesy of the Missouri Historical Society)

THIS USED TO BE: An 1890s Burlesque Theater

NOW IT'S: Walnut Street at 7th Street

LOCATION: Downtown St. Louis

10

Drury Inn & Suites Convention Center

Two-story arches filled with ornamental grills, oculus windows, and bands of ornamental terra-cotta highlight the walls of the Drury Inn Convention Center. The Drury chain, known for its attentive care and healthy happy hours, converted a historic public market to create this 178-room hotel adjacent to the America's Center.

Public markets like Union Market, with scores of stalls leased out to individual vendors, were an essential part of city life during the nineteenth and early twentieth centuries. The city of St. Louis set aside property in growing neighborhoods for markets and built the first Union Market building on this site in 1866. In the original Union Market building, wild game, cheeses, bakery goods, and vats of sauerkraut were available for sale. The market's location on the northern edge of downtown—adjacent to crowded residential communities that were filled with waves of Irish, Polish, Russian, and Italian immigrants—assured that the market would be thronged with customers all day.

In 1925, the city constructed a new, block-sized Union Market building, celebrated as "the second largest enclosed market in the world."[5] While displays of fruits, vegetables, meats, and edibles of all kinds filled the first floor, the upper floors were a public garage.

As demand for public markets reduced with the rise of grocery store chains in the mid-twentieth century, much of the market space was converted into a garage for cross-country and public service buses. In 1990, Drury Inn & Suites, a chain dedicated to saving historic buildings by converting them into hotels, turned the then vacant market building into the Drury Inn & Suites Convention Center.

The new Union Market building as it appeared when it opened in 1925. (Postcard from a private collection)

THIS USED TO BE: Union Market

NOW IT'S: Drury Inn & Suites Convention Center

LOCATION: 711 North Broadway

11

Bailey's Range and Apartments

The building facing Olive Street at 9th Street that houses the popular Bailey's Range and floors of apartments was built to house the high-tech business of its day—the Bell Telephone Company. With its rough-cut red sandstone, its deep red brick, and its Roman arched windows, the seven-story building looks like the corner of a castle. Adding to its medieval character, the brick corbeling at the cornice forms a series of Roman arches. Though Romanesque buildings were common throughout downtown during the 1890s, the building at 920 Olive Street is one of only a few extant.

It was built by the Bell Telephone Company in 1889, years before long-distance lines opened between St. Louis and Kansas City and between St. Louis and New York on June 24, 1896.

Three extensive phone companies—one operating in Missouri, Kansas, and Arkansas, another in Oklahoma, and the third in Texas—were formally merged in April 1920. The resulting Southwestern Bell Telephone was based in St. Louis, with its offices at 920 Olive.

The booming business soon outgrew its little castle on Olive. The company opened its new, Art Deco office building, the 1010 Pine Building, in 1926. A skyscraper, 1010 Pine stood 369 feet tall.

The thriving S. G. Adams business and office supplies company filled 920 Olive for decades. As part of the rebirth of downtown's residential community at the turn of the millennium, the then historic building was renovated as apartments with first-floor commercial space.

After the tornado of May 10, 1896 ripped away the telephone lines, halting communications during the crisis, the lines in downtown were re-installed underground.

The Romanesque Bell Telephone Building as it originally appeared. Telephone poles like the ones shown on the Olive Street side of the building lined downtown's sidewalks. (Illustration courtesy of the Carondelet Historical Society)

THIS USED TO BE: Bell Telephone Building

NOW IT'S: Bailey's Range and Apartments

LOCATION: 920 Olive Boulevard

Market Street from 18th to 20th Streets

Expansive Aloe Plaza, the park facing Union Station, is the stage of the stunning Milles Fountain. Officially named *The Meeting of the Waters*, it depicts the confluence of the Missouri and the Mississippi Rivers. The great Swedish sculptor Carl Milles created the fountain with fourteen bronze figures in a giant rectangular pool of black and salmon marble. When it was unveiled in 1940, the fountain's male and female figures were so provocative that they stirred a short-lived controversy.

During the mid-nineteenth century, a middle-class residential neighborhood filled the site of the plaza. Rows of dignified town houses with white stone steps lined the streets. Gradually, industries encroached on the blocks. Handsome row houses became dilapidated tenements. The neighborhood degenerated into part of a district known as the Bottoms, or the Bad Lands, or Death Valley. The boundaries varied through the years, but the district encompassed the subtle valley (now disguised by highway ramps) that extended along Market and Chestnut Streets west to about Jefferson Avenue.

By the turn of the century, saloons, honky-tonks, gambling dens, and brothels filled the district. Gangs ruled the streets—including the Bottoms Gang, the Chestnut Gang, and Egan's Rats. Hooligans terrorized shopkeepers. Gangs harassed senior citizens, and gang rapes terrorized women. Gangs even cornered a musician on his way home from work and smashed his violin over his head.

Death Valley was compared to the most notorious and dangerous districts in American cities—the Bowery in New York, the Creole quarter in New Orleans, and San Francisco's Barbary Coast.

After the passage of a bond issue for civic improvements in 1923, the urban landscape along Market Street was transformed block by block into a ribbon of parkway eventually stretching from 12th to 21st Streets. The Milles Fountain and surrounding parkway, framed by impressive buildings, erased the memory of rowdy, rundown, and notorious Death Valley.

Art Frank penned a three-verse poem that vividly describes the lawlessness in Death Valley during the 1890s. The last verse depicts the sounds and sights of the valley and the violence that ruled its streets:

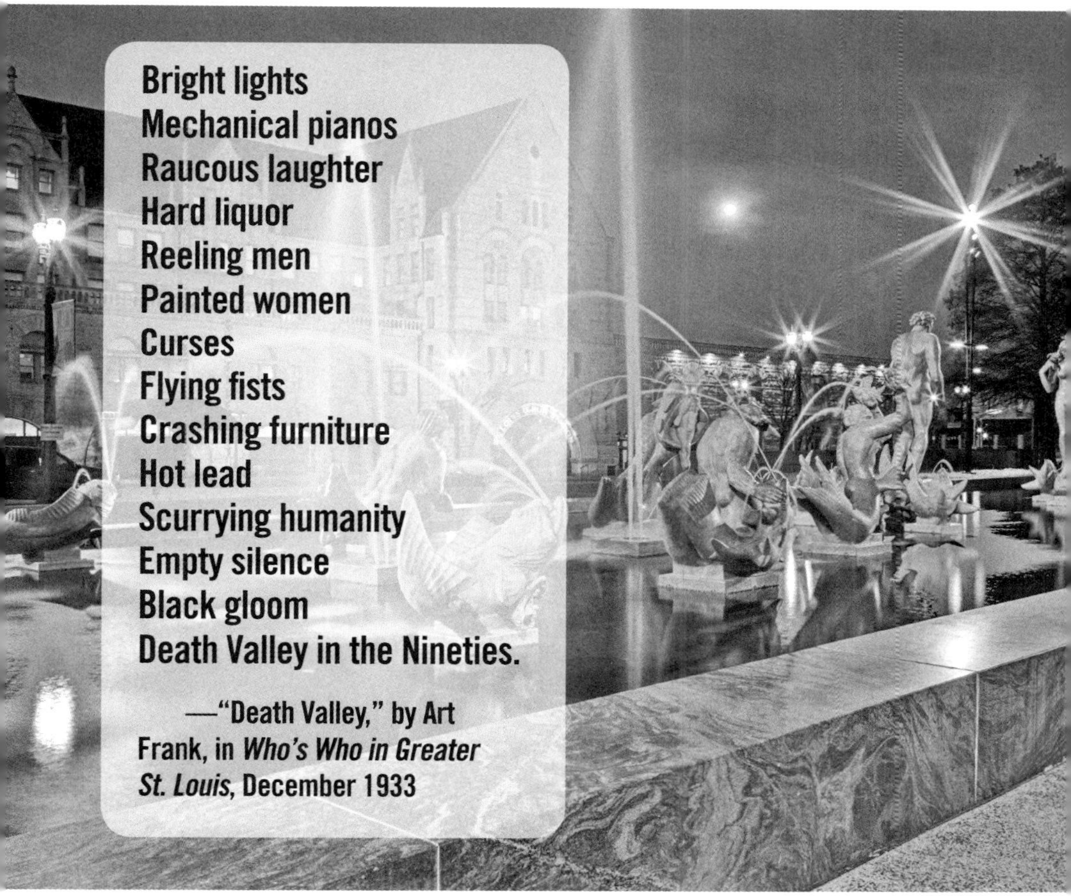

Bright lights
Mechanical pianos
Raucous laughter
Hard liquor
Reeling men
Painted women
Curses
Flying fists
Crashing furniture
Hot lead
Scurrying humanity
Empty silence
Black gloom
Death Valley in the Nineties.

—"Death Valley," by Art Frank, in *Who's Who in Greater St. Louis*, December 1933

THIS USED TO BE: Death Valley

NOW IT'S: Aloe Plaza

LOCATION: Market Street from 18th to 20th Streets

2020 Washington Condominiums

When this eight-story factory at 2020 Washington Avenue was converted into 103 fashionable loft-style condominiums, the building was described as the former home of the *Sporting News*.

The weekly publication, founded in 1886 and known as the "baseball bible," moved its operations into the factory in the late 1940s. (The *Sporting News* was sold to the Times Mirror Company in 1977.) The building, however, had played a significant role in the St. Louis economy long before it housed the sports publication.

Emerson Electric Company constructed the factory with 150,000 square feet in 1919–20. Light gray brick with Bedford stone trim sheathed the walls of the $600,000 factory.

The entrance to the condominiums in the former Emerson Electric factory at 2020 Washington Avenue (Photo by NiNi Harris)

The factory's scale reflected the tremendous growth of this St. Louis business, which was incorporated in 1890 to manufacture electrical specialties. The company focused on small motors and began producing fans and eventually the Emerson ceiling fan, often called the Casablanca fan. The successful company kept growing and moving to larger spaces in downtown. In 1919, Emerson employed twelve hundred workers in the manufacture of small motors and fans. During the last four months of that year, the company was said to have refused orders totaling three

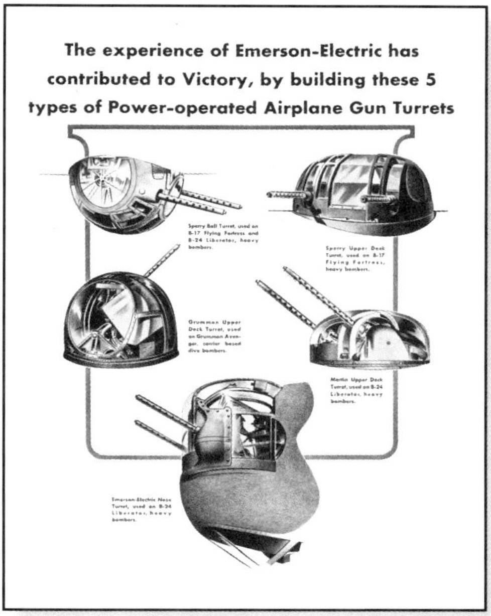

An illustration showing gun turrets produced by Emerson Electric during World War II for B-17 and B-24 bombers. (Illustration from a private collection)

million dollars due to lack of capacity.

The new eight-story factory at 2020 Washington enabled Emerson Electric to increase production and employ another thousand workers.

During World War II, Emerson Electric's plants produced the turrets for the gunners on the US Army Air Force's heavy bombers—the B-17 Flying Fortress and B-24 Liberator. The ball turrets enabled the gunners to maneuver so they could shoot at the enemy fighters coming from any direction. These turrets saved the lives of many American flight crews and hastened the end of the war.

Following World War II, Emerson moved its downtown operations to its North County campus.

THIS USED TO BE: Emerson Electric's Ball Turret Factory

NOW IT'S: Condominiums

LOCATION: 2020 Washington

Washington Avenue Loft District

The neighborhood energy on Washington Avenue seems to almost bubble up from the sidewalk. The Bankers Lofts building at 9th Street and Washington Avenue anchors the east end of the Washington Avenue loft district, and the 2020 Washington building marks the western end. Coffee shops, bars, convenience stores, and restaurants fill the first-floor storefronts of the giant brick, stone, and terra-cotta warehouses lining the street. These magnificent warehouses that have been converted into apartments and condominiums are home to thousands of St. Louisans.

This vibrant residential district was once known as "Shoe Street USA." During the 1920s, more shoe trade was carried on along Washington Avenue than on any other street in the world.

The A. D. Brown Building on Washington at Tucker Boulevard was built in 1897 for the Hamilton-Brown Shoe Company. Four years later, the eight-story warehouse on Washington at 13th Street was constructed for Peters Shoe. And in 1910, German American architect Theodore Link designed the International Shoe Building at 1501 Washington.

These huge buildings are monuments to an industry that grew in St. Louis with the industrial revolution. During that era, the manufacturing of shoes moved from small shops to bigger and bigger factories.

On the eve of World War II, ten thousand St. Louisans were working in the shoe industry, Anheuser-Busch was growing, and the St. Louis Browns were continuing their losing ways in the American League. St. Louis truly was, as the saying went, "First in shoes, first in booze, and last in the American League."

Bustling Washington Avenue—lined with giant dry goods stores, warehouses, and shoe factories—in 1909. (Postcard from a private collection)

The Civil War had boosted the St. Louis shoe trade, and in the decade from 1883 to 1893 the number of shoes produced in St. Louis increased from a half million to four and a half million pairs. By 1905, St. Louis ranked third in the nation in shoe production. In 1911, the merger of two local shoe companies—Peters Shoe Company and Roberts, Johnson & Rand Company—led to greater efficiency and increased production.

By 1929, annual production of shoes in St. Louis had risen to 87 million pairs.

THIS USED TO BE: "Shoe Street USA"

NOW IT'S: Washington Avenue Loft District

LOCATION: Downtown St. Louis

15

Ely Walker Lofts

The huge building at 1520 Washington Avenue is filled with 174 luxury loft-style apartments ranging from 1,000 to 1,600 square feet. The lavish terra-cotta trim on the exterior of the seven-story building belies its original use as a warehouse for a dry goods company. A powerhouse of a business, Ely, Walker & Company Dry Goods resulted from the business acumen of an adopted St. Louisan and created the initial wealth for a family that spawned generations of local civic leaders and a national political dynasty.

Its story began with the arrival of David Davis Walker in St. Louis in 1857. The college-educated Illinois farm boy started as an office boy with a local wholesale dry goods house, where he rose to the position of partner in only eight years. In 1880, he formed Ely, Walker & Co. with Frank Ely. The company became the leading dry goods wholesaler west of the Mississippi River. In 1906, they built the massive warehouse at 1520 Washington Avenue.

D. D. Walker's son George Herbert Walker was a heavyweight boxing champion who worked for the family business before starting G. H. Walker & Co. in 1900. His banking and investment company quickly prospered and bought and sold the New Orleans, Texas & Mexico Railway and the Laclede Gas Co.

His daughter Dorothy, after attending finishing school, met Yale graduate and World War I army captain Prescott Bush, who had come to St. Louis to work for a local hardware company. A month after her twentieth birthday, Dorothy and Prescott married. The next year they had their first son, Prescott Jr. Two years later, they named their second son George Herbert Walker Bush. He would become the 41st president of the United States, and his son George Walker Bush became the forty-third president of the United States.

Proprietors of general stores throughout the Midwest and West made annual buying trips to St. Louis to examine and order household goods from the Ely, Walker & Co. warehouse on Washington Avenue.

Ely Walker Lofts. (Photo by Don Korte)

Displays of wholesale goods in the Ely Walker building on Washington Avenue in the 1950s. (Courtesy of the Missouri Historical Society)

THIS USED TO BE: Dry Goods Company That Spawned a Political Dynasty

NOW IT'S: Ely Walker Lofts

LOCATION: 1520 Washington Avenue

16

Schlafly Tap Room

The Schlafly Tap Room, with its brick-walled courtyard, recalls medieval Europe. Its huge Tudor arched windows are framed by molded brick. The ceramic tile roof forms Flemish-style stepped gables. The subtleties in the brickwork—its irregular textures, its warm colors, the patterns in how the bricks were laid—add to its ancient feel.

Inside, giant timbers support wood joists. The wide plank floors are laid at angles. Tables and chairs fill the rooms, and it seems every room offers views of giant brew kettles and tanks.

The Schlafly Tap Room received the first microbrewery license issued by the state of Missouri and officially opened in this setting on December 26, 1991. Its building, which feels like a historic beer hall, was built for a radically different use—the home of the Lambert-Deacon-Hull Printing Company.

Partners Arthur W. Lambert and Richard Deacon, both active in the management of Lambert Pharmacal Company, and experienced printer James Hull chose self-taught architect Samuel Scherer to design the new printing company's complex. Scherer, a student of the art of printing, later became director of the Saint Louis Art Museum. He designed two adjoining buildings, completed in 1902 and 1904, that form the U-shaped complex around the Tap Room's courtyard.

For seventy-five years, the building housed heavy printing presses, which explains the huge steel beams that are mostly disguised by the ubiquitous wood. In 1939, the name of the second printing company to occupy the building, "John S. Swift Company, Planographers, Printers," was written in gold in the terra-cotta panel over the door.

The Romanesque building of red brick and red sandstone at 2101 Locust (across the street from the Tap Room) was built in 1891 as the home of the Lambert Pharmacal Company, manufacturers of Listerine.

The alternating glazed brick creates designs in the walls of the entrance to the Schlafly Tap Room. (Photo by Dylan Weber Callahan)

THIS USED TO BE: Printing Company

NOW IT'S: Schlafly Tap Room

LOCATION: 2100 Locust Street

17

The Fountain on Locust

The Fountain on Locust, known for its flamboyant Art Deco interior, is a popular destination for its specialty desserts like rum raisin ice cream (topped with a shot of rum) and its signature ice cream martinis. While the Fountain opened in 2008, the two-story building housing the restaurant dates to 1916. With its stucco facade and ornate baroque trim, the building reflects Hollywood's Mission Revival style as seen in the silent movies of that era.

A century ago, the expansive first-floor windows of the restaurant building, which today allow customers to watch the foot traffic as they enjoy exotic fountain treats, were display windows that showcased sport sedans. In 1918, the Supreme Motor Company, a Stutz dealer, operated in the storefront. Indianapolis-based Stutz was known for its early race cars. Popular models included the sporty Jazz Age Stutz Bearcat and the luxury Stutz Blackhawk.

The Mission Revival building was home to the dealership until 1924. Later it housed Nash, Buick, and Chevrolet dealerships.

During the early twentieth century, 3037 Locust was at the heart of the old Automobile Row, which stretched from about 17th Street to Grand Avenue. In the era before car lots, the row housed auto dealerships, distributorships, and auto supply companies. During its heyday, Automobile Row had an aura of stylishness as customers strolled along urban sidewalks window shopping for the latest models.

As the dealerships moved out of urban storefronts to large lots on wide streets, new businesses filled the buildings. During the mid-twentieth century, a chemical company, a brokerage firm, and even the Coca-Cola Bottling Company's advertising department occupied the Mission Revival treasure.

Despite the Great Depression's erosion of the market for glamorous cars, Stutz continued to manufacture its Jazz Age automobiles until 1935.

Baroque-style terra-cotta decorates the facade of the Fountain on Locust. (Photo by Dylan Weber Callahan)

THIS USED TO BE: An Automobile Dealership

NOW IT'S: The Fountain on Locust

LOCATION: 3037 Locust

Saint Louis University's Campus East of Grand

Saint Louis University's English Gothic–style, white stone church (the College Church) and its red-brick nineteenth-century halls line the west side of Grand Avenue at Lindell Boulevard. These Victorian-era buildings face mid-century modern and early twenty-first-century campus halls, a student union, and athletic fields on the east side of Grand. On the site of this newer campus area east of Grand, the fate of St. Louis and perhaps the fate of the nation was decided in the spring of 1861.

At the beginning of the Civil War, eight hundred state militia, who wanted to secede from the Union, established their camp at Lindell Grove (the campus east of Grand). They named their camp in honor of Missouri governor Claiborne Fox Jackson, who also supported seceding from the Union. Their immediate goal was to take control of the federal arsenal in South City, which housed enough muskets, gun powder, cartridges, and cannon to equip a small rebel army.

Through the winter and spring of 1861, citizens who supported the Union, mostly German, had been secretly drilling in breweries, factories, and in the Turner Hall (a German gymnasium). Individuals and business leaders had been surreptitiously providing uniforms and muskets to these citizens committed to saving the Union. Known as the Home Guard, they were determined to protect the arsenal. The Home Guard planned a preemptive move on Camp Jackson, eliminating the immediate threat posed by the state militia.

During the Civil War, Saint Louis University was located on Washington Avenue at 9th Street in downtown. The Jesuits began to move the campus to Midtown at Grand and Lindell in the late 1880s.

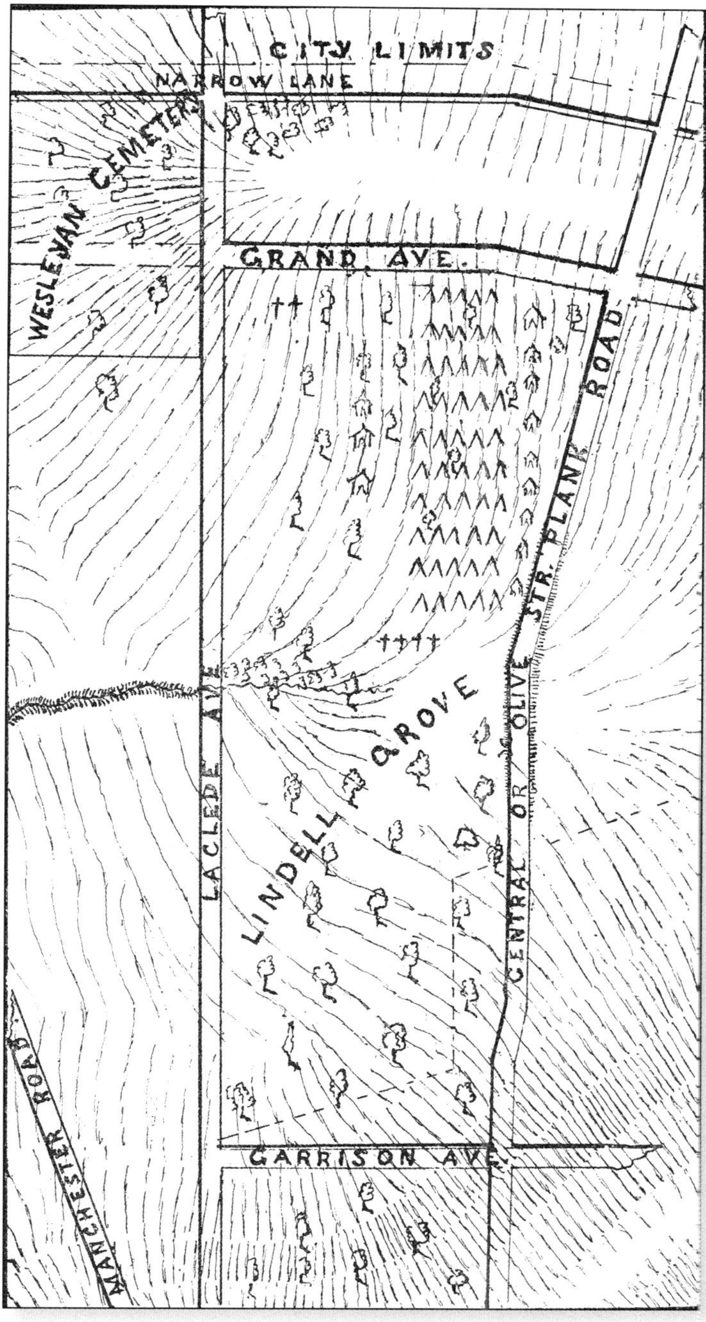

Hand-drawn sketch of Camp Jackson from Robert Julius Rombauer's *The Union Cause in St. Louis in 1861: An Historical Sketch*. Rombauer had fled to America and then settled in St. Louis after the failed Hungarian Revolution of 1848. He and his brothers served in the Union army. (From a private collection)

On the morning of May 10, these uniformed and armed Union volunteers gathered at secret locations in North and South City and then marched in regiments through the streets to downtown St. Louis. The seven thousand volunteer soldiers must have shocked the rest of the population. From downtown, they marched west on Olive Street, Market, Pine, and Laclede Avenue. They surrounded Camp Jackson. Without a fight, the secessionist state militia surrendered to the overwhelming number of Union volunteers.

Later, as these untested Union volunteers marched their prisoners back toward downtown on Olive Street, angry Confederate sympathizers taunted and hurled rocks at them. A shot was fired, and a Union captain fell, mortally wounded. The Union volunteers responded, firing at the unruly mob on the streets. Twenty-eight were killed in what became known as the Battle of Camp Jackson. The community was horrified.

The Battle of Camp Jackson was seared into the memory of St. Louisans not just because of civilian deaths in the street, but because it marked a turning point. The German volunteers had shocked the community with their numbers and their dedication to the Union. With one show of force on May 10, 1861, German St. Louisans had changed the character and culture of the city and made it clear that St. Louis would be a Union city.

The secessionist crowd yelled ethnic slurs at the Home Guard, intending to deride the German volunteers as the damned Deutsch. Instead they shouted the "damned Dutch," resulting in St. Louis Germans being called "Dutch" for generations.

Troops gather in the foreground of Camp Jackson. The militia's tents were in the northwest quadrant of the grove, near Grand and Lindell. (Photo courtesy of the Archives of Saint Louis University's Pius XII Memorial Library)

THIS USED TO BE: Lindell Grove, the Campsite of the Secessionists

NOW IT'S: Saint Louis University's Campus

LOCATION: Mid Town

City House in Grand Center Arts District

Charming City House is wedged between theaters, offices, large apartment buildings, and venues in the thriving Grand Center Arts District. The district boasts twelve thousand theater seats located within four blocks. Some of its museums, galleries, and arts organizations occupy historic buildings that have classical styling. Others, like the Pulitzer and the Contemporary Art Museum St. Louis, boast new, wildly contemporary buildings that make concrete look gorgeous.

City House is the oldest remaining building in Grand Center. (Photo by Brian Kolde)

In the midst of these grand-scaled buildings that make powerful architectural statements, the dollhouse-like, Second Empire–style City House recalls that Grand Center was once a fashionable residential neighborhood. City House, constructed in 1874, is the oldest remaining building in Grand Center.

In the years following the Civil War, residential development spread west from downtown. By 1875, clusters of two- and three-story town houses and row houses stood

Grand Center Inc., founded in 1981, has established Grand Center as the cultural and arts center of St. Louis.

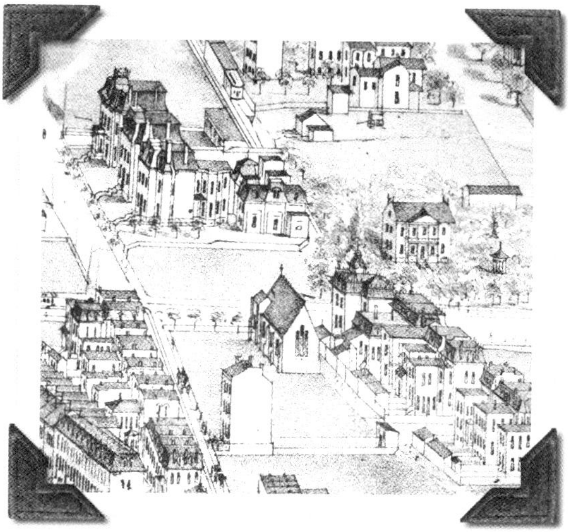

Pictorial St. Louis shows scattered clusters of town houses, the first generation of development in Midtown's Grand Center, in 1875. (Illustration courtesy of Carondelet Historical Society)

along Olive Street, Washington Avenue, and Lindell Boulevard as far west as Grand Avenue. The horsecar line from downtown reached Grand and Olive, which spurred more development, spilling west of Grand.

After the streetcars were electrified, increasing foot traffic, a second generation of development replaced the fashionable nineteenth-century residences with huge office buildings and theaters. Other gracious town houses were converted for commercial use. Midtown was transformed into a second downtown.

Following World War II, the growth of the suburbs gradually drained the businesses from Midtown St. Louis. The theater seats were left empty. The charming, historic home at 3534 Washington Avenue was abandoned. It was just one of many buildings in Grand Center that fell into disrepair.

In 1990, Grand Center Inc. acquired the property and transferred it to attorney Paul R. Hales, who exquisitely restored City House as his law office.

THIS USED TO BE: An elegant home in a Victorian-era residential neighborhood

NOW IT'S: City House in Grand Center Arts District

LOCATION: 3534 Washington Avenue

Saint Louis University's Office of Admissions

During the late 1970s, part of the student experience at Saint Louis University was being approached by a missionary from the Church of Scientology. The missionaries came from the castle-like mansion neighboring the university that was owned by the Church of Scientology from 1974 to 1985. The mysterious white stone mansion on Lindell Boulevard had towers, turrets, dormer windows, and bay windows.

The mansion dates to 1890, when grand homes lined Lindell at Grand Avenue. English immigrant Alexander Euston, who made his fortune in the white lead and oil business, had built the stone castle at 3730 Lindell that boasted sixteen rooms and a ballroom. The interior was lush with ornate molded plaster, stained glass, onyx mantles, and hand-carved hardwoods.

A St. Louis–based religious society, the Daughters of the Queen of Heaven, bought the grand home in 1912 and converted it into a boardinghouse for single women. Homes operated by religious organizations provided comfortable and safe environments for single working women, many of whom had moved to St. Louis from rural areas or small towns. In 1947, residents at the Queen's Daughters Home paid six to ten dollars per week for room and board. The Queen's Daughters ran the working woman's home until 1972.

Original Victorian-era hardware on the mansion of Alexander Euston. (Photo by Brian Kolde)

In 1988, Saint Louis University—which has incorporated recycled mid-century modern office buildings, convents, and Victorian-era residences into the institution's Midtown

The stonework of the mansion at 3730 Lindell Boulevard is a testament to the wealth of its builder, English immigrant and businessman Alexander Euston. (Photo by Brian Kolde)

campus—acquired the mansion. The university renovated the Lindell Boulevard mansion as Saint Louis University's spectacular Office of Admissions.

THIS USED TO BE: The Church of Scientology and the Queen's Daughters Residence

NOW IT'S: Saint Louis University's Office of Admissions

LOCATION: 3730 Lindell Boulevard

Saint Louis University Museum of Art

Generations of Saint Louis University students knew the palatial building opposite the campus on Lindell Boulevard as the regional headquarters of the F. W. Woolworth Corporation. With its mansard roof, cartouches over the windows, French doors, balustrades, and ornamental brackets, its elegance was unlike that of any other office building.

The imitation French palace, however, was not built as a corporate headquarters. The exclusive St. Louis Club built the three-story French Renaissance building in 1901. The club's amenities included a basement swimming pool, a top-floor ballroom, and a spectacular four-story staircase. In this lavish setting, the St. Louis Club's members enjoyed fabulous New Year's Eve parties.

The club's palace on Lindell cost $320,000 to build. It was designed by Joseph Freedlander and Arthur Dillon, two recent graduates of the École des Beaux-Arts. Though their fledgling firm was based in New York, Dillon was rooted in St. Louis. His father was the managing editor of the *Post-Dispatch*, and his uncle by marriage was the great bridge builder James B. Eads.

Fire ravaged the building in 1925. Renovated as offices, the club building became home to an insurance company and then served as the F. W. Woolworth Company regional offices.

The third floor of the Saint Louis University Museum of Art is dedicated to the nineteenth-century history of the Jesuits in mid-America. Among the artifacts that Jesuit frontiersman, missionary, and author Pierre-Jean DeSmet brought from Europe for the Jesuit missions are seventeenth-century globes by the great Dutch mapmaker, Willem Blaeu.

This card, postmarked 1913, shows the French-inspired Saint Louis University Museum of Art when it was still home to the St. Louis Club. (Postcard from a private collection)

Palatial details on the Saint Louis University Museum of Art. (Photo by Brian Kolde)

Saint Louis University bought the former St. Louis Club building and restored it as the university's museum of art. Thanks to that thoughtful restoration, the entrance hall and staircase again glitter with Art Nouveau styling.

THIS USED TO BE: St. Louis Club and F. W. Woolworth Offices

NOW IT'S: Saint Louis University Museum of Art

LOCATION: 3663 Lindell Boulevard

The House at 4232 McPherson Avenue

A simple two-and-a-half-story brick house with a gabled roof and gabled porch sits on a long block of McPherson Avenue. The house, in the midst of both historic buildings and new urban-style residences, is remarkably restrained for turn-of-the-century St. Louis architecture.

When this dignified house was still new, it was home to a St. Louis woman whose lifestyle and writings were unorthodox. From 1903 to 1904, Kate Chopin lived here with her five adult sons. She smoked, rode horseback, held weekly salons, and wrote stories for national magazines. In 1898, the publication of her controversial novel *The Awakening* brought disapproval. This story of a married woman in love with another man was criticized as "morbid" and even "vulgar," and it was banned from some local libraries.

Chopin's personal experiences had given texture and depth to both *The Awakening*, which brought condemnation, and to her short stories, which captured the subtleties of Louisiana's Creole culture. Born in St. Louis in 1851, she grew up in the family home near the present site of Busch Stadium. Her mother was a descendent of early St. Louis Creoles and her father was a successful Irish American businessman. In 1870, she married New Orleans cotton trader Oscar Chopin and moved to his family's plantation in Louisiana. When her husband unexpectedly died, the thirty-two-year-old widow was left with six children and business debts. She entered a man's world to manage her deceased husband's business interests out of debt. After succeeding, she moved back to St. Louis in 1884 to be near her ailing mother and where her children could take advantage of St. Louis's outstanding school system. Chopin began writing for Harper's and Century magazines. While writing for prestigious publications, her touching stories of Creole life in the South, *Bayou Folk* was published in 1894.

During the summer of 1904, she enjoyed her new home's proximity to the World's Fair. After a long summer day spent at the Fair, Kate Chopin took ill. She died two days later, August 22, in her home on McPherson. Her death was attributed to a cerebral hemorrhage.

Kate Chopin's home at 4232 McPherson. (Photo by Brian Kolde)

St. Louis native and author Kate Chopin in her Victorian riding gear. Other than *Bayou Folk*, her collection of haunting stories of Creole life in the South, Chopin's work fell into obscurity for decades. (Photo courtesy of the Missouri Historical Society)

In the 1970s, feminism propelled the rediscovery of Chopin's writings. Her works have been translated into Albanian, Czech, Vietnamese, and a dozen other languages.

THIS USED TO BE: The Home of Feminist Author Kate Chopin

NOW IT'S: A Private Home

LOCATION: 4232 McPherson Avenue

23

Pulitzer Arts Foundation Offices

The three-story dark-brick building at 3737 Washington Avenue in Grand Center serves as offices of the Pulitzer Arts Foundation, the brainchild of Emily Rauh Pulitzer and Joseph Pulitzer Jr., which presents experimental and progressive programs. Terra-cotta panels with garland patterns highlight the brick facade of the foundation's otherwise austere office building.

The building was constructed in 1902 as a club and home for wealthy, professional bachelors. The club took the name Pendennis from a character in William Thackeray's novel *Major Pendennis*, who had become synonymous with bachelorhood.

Each of the club building's floors had three apartments with baths. A common room on each floor offered a setting for socializing and breakfast with other club members. The club gave bachelors an alternative to living in their family homes or residing in a hotel.

On December 15, 1911, a front-page *Post-Dispatch* account of a small fire at the club was filled with innuendo. Early that morning, the bachelors had attempted to put out a fire that had started in "the attic above the apartments of Eugene H. Angert, lawyer, wit and after-dinner speaker," the *Post* reported. The headline read, "Bachelors Parade in Pajamas at Apartment Blaze. . . . RAINBOW IS OUTDONE. Baby Blue, Mauve. Lavender and Stripes in Robe de Nuit Color Scheme." The article ridiculed the prominent men who had tried to douse the fire while in their nightclothes. Chemist and engineer William M. Chauvenet was reported as wearing "a charming creation of baby blue," and Washington University professor O. S. James wore "a conservative, but abbreviated lavender toilet." Another member, "in a diaphonous two-piece suit," manned a garden hose.[6]

Despite the bachelors' bucket brigade, the fire was gaining when the firemen arrived. The professional firefighters efficiently saved the building, but the club never fully recovered from the ridicule. In 1937, the last club members sold the building, and for years it was a regular apartment building.

The handsome turn-of-the-century offices of the Pulitzer Arts Foundation. (Photo by Brian Kolde)

THIS USED TO BE: A Bachelor Club

NOW IT'S: Pulitzer Arts Foundation Offices

LOCATION: 3737 Washington

The IBEW's Henry Miller Museum

In 1891, this row house with first-floor storefronts was the scene of discussions and negotiations between dedicated men who helped transform the lives of working-class Americans.

The building (constructed during the mid-nineteenth century with grainy, handmade St. Louis brick) was humble. John Greb ran his saloon in the first-floor storefront. Electrician Henry Miller boarded on the second floor. Waves of immigrants from Russia, Ireland, Germany, and Sicily were crowded into the surrounding neighborhood. Streetcar tracks followed busy Franklin Avenue, later renamed Dr. Martin Luther King Drive.

At that time, electrical workers from around the nation were working in St. Louis on an exposition. Henry Miller listened to their stories of hazardous work, lack of training, long hours, and minimal pay. In response, he helped organize electrical workers' locals. And in the second-floor boardinghouse rooms, Miller and nine like-minded leaders from around the country formed the International Brotherhood of Electrical Workers (IBEW) and wrote its constitution.

That profound event in the Franklin Avenue boardinghouse went unnoticed at the time, but 125 years later the IBEW numbers more than 725,000 members.

The building at 2726–28 Franklin Avenue and the surrounding commercial street would go through many incarnations in subsequent years. The west storefront of the row house was used as a saloon up until Prohibition outlawed liquor, then it became a restaurant operated by Greek Americans, and in the mid-1920s Polish-born and Russian-speaking Benjamin Iken opened a grocery store in it.

The IBEW carefully restored the building and opened it as a museum, sacred to the working people of the United States, in time for the 125th anniversary of the brotherhood in the fall of 2016.

The mid-nineteenth century building at 2726–28 Dr. Martin Luther King Drive has been restored as the Henry Miller Museum. (Photo by Emma Prince)

The east storefront became the home of the Wah Leo Hop Laundry in 1915. In 1924, a Yiddish-speaking Russian immigrant and naturalized citizen named Abraham Zimmerman turned the laundry space into a harness shop. He later made the transition to early twentieth-century markets, turning his shop into Abraham Zimmerman Shoes.

Following World War II, the neighborhood suffered a severe decline, and 2726–28 Franklin was neglected for decades. When Local 1 of the IBEW bought the property in 2015, the row house with first-floor storefronts was almost collapsing.

THIS USED TO BE: A Chinese Laundry and a Russian Immigrant's Harness Shop

NOW IT'S: The IBEW's Henry Miller Museum

LOCATION: 2726–28 Dr. Martin Luther King Drive

25

The Caramel Room

The top floor of the massive brick warehouse in the old industrial district along North Broadway has been the venue for elegant weddings and parties. Known as The Caramel Room, this venue features century-old hardwood floors, exposed brick walls, wildly contemporary chandeliers, and wall-sized windows offering spectacular views of the river and of the Stan Musial Bridge.

Taking the elevator to the third story, visitors used to enter a glass-walled room looking down on the spotless factory floor. There, white-uniformed craftsmen, wearing garb appropriate for an operating room, were creating the ultimate confections—chocolate-covered blackberries, glaceed apricots au chocolat, chocolate-covered wine grapes, and chocolate caramels. They mixed small batches in copper kettles. The craftsmen used the recipes passed down in the Bissinger family, which began its storied tradition of crafting confections in seventeenth-century France. The treasured delicacies produced by these talented confectioners were carefully packaged and then shipped to chocolate lovers across the country.

Except for the name Bissinger's in old-world script at the top of the building, nothing about the outside of the massive brick warehouse on a stone foundation suggested its use. Nor did it suggest that the top floor had been transformed into a breath taking event space. And nothing indicated the building's original purpose.

The warehouse at 1600 North Broadway was built in 1910 for the Missouri, Kansas & Texas (Katy) Railroad. (Though the railroad originally formed at the end of the Civil War to serve more states, by 1870 investors focused on traffic to Kansas and Texas, resulting in the Katy name.) The trains could roll into the back side of the cavernous

An eleven million dollar renovation transformed the neglected warehouse into Bissinger's Handcrafted Chocolatiers—with eighty-five thousand square feet for production, storage, corporate offices, and an event space.

In May 1911, the *St. Louis Realty Record & Builder* stated that the new Missouri, Kansas & Texas Railway freight depot marked "a new epoch in shipping facilities of St. Louis." (Courtesy of Carondelet Historical Society)

warehouse that provided internal switches and loading docks with two levels of storage space.

In the 1980s, the railroad sold 1600 North Broadway. Used for storage, the railroad warehouse deteriorated until its purchase by Bissinger's. Then the St. Louis-based Chocolate Chocolate Chocolate Company acquired Bissinger's in 2019, and continues to run the Bissinger brand. While the production of Bissenger's confections with the historic recipes and fine ingredients was moved to the plant of Chocolate Chocolate Chocolate on The Hill, The Caramel Room continues to host glamorous events on North Broadway.

THIS USED TO BE: The Katy Railroad Warehouse

NOW IT'S: The Caramel Room Event Space

LOCATION: 1600 North Broadway

Vacant Lot at 4460 Delmar Boulevard

Today, not even a faint clue exists of the political influence once wielded as the backdrop of energetic music played in the nightclub that once stood on the vacant lot at 4460 Delmar. Few cars travel the now quiet block of Delmar that has more vacant lots than buildings. In its heyday, however, the block thronged with crowds when Duke Ellington, Ella Fitzgerald, and Nat King Cole performed for full houses at the Riviera Nightclub, considered the best African American nightclub in the Midwest. The club also served as the base of political operations for Jordan W. Chambers, known as the "Negro mayor of St. Louis." Chambers, who operated a funeral parlor in addition to the club, developed a strong grassroots political organization in the city's Nineteenth Ward. That ward boasted fourteen thousand voters.

Each evening, after Chambers received citizens at his funeral parlor and listened to their problems and ideas, he went to the club. *Post-Dispatch* columnist Ralph Coghlan described it as "a mecca of local Negroes." There, Chambers, "sees many other people. The cocktail bar on the lower floor of the club is often turned into a kind of debating society. . . . Pops, as the youngsters call him, listens to argument and dispenses wisdom. 'Some nights,' said Pops, 'you might see three or four Negro Ph.Ds at the bar.'" Coghlan described the club as "a kind of intellectual center."[7]

As he came and went from the Riviera, Chambers was instantly recognizable in his uniform white Stetson hat and black string tie, and he often puffed on a pipe filled with heavily scented tobacco. Candidates and politicians sought his support and advice. Yet, with the exception of political leaders, he was almost unknown in the white community.

After Chambers's death, the Riviera club became the home of a fraternal organization. It burned in 1970.

EXECUTIVE COMMITTEE

Left to Right—Front Row: Harold W. Ross, Thelma M. Grant, T. D. McNeal, Jordan W. Chambers, Atty. John A. Davis; Rear Row: Columbus Ewing, Leyton Weston, Atty. David M. Grant and Judge Geo. L. Vaughn.

I AM 100% BEHIND THE PROGRAM . . .

. . . of the . . .

March On Washington Committee

LON THOMAS

1818 NORTH TAYLOR FRanklin 8894

2

Jordan W. Chambers (front row fourth from the left) dressed as his fellow committee members for the March On Washington movement. The movement called for greater opportunities for African Americans to advance in the defense industries. (Photo courtesy of the Missouri Historical Society)

When Jordan Chambers unexpectedly died on August 11, 1962, United States senators sent their sympathies. A telegram from former president Harry S. Truman stated that he regretted "the loss of a first class citizen."

THIS USED TO BE: Riviera Nightclub

NOW IT'S: Vacant Lot

LOCATION: 4460 Delmar Boulevard

27

A Contemporary Urban Forest

Chain-link fencing surrounds a young oak and hickory forest growing among chunks of building debris from the failed Pruitt-Igoe housing complex. The young urban forest covers much of the fifty-seven-acre Pruitt-Igoe site just northwest of downtown, framed roughly by 20th and Carr Streets and Cass and Jefferson Avenues. Other parts of the acreage are neatly maintained grounds of schools and a soccer field. A modern-style library built in 1953 and now used as a church is a remnant of the time when the crowded public housing high-rises filled this acreage.

These acres were developed as the Pruitt-Igoe housing project in the mid-twentieth century. Thirty blocks of an aging neighborhood had been cleared to build the high-rises. The skeletons of the Pruitt-Igoe towers were already five stories tall when the national commissioner of the Public Housing Administration visited St. Louis to see the progress. The *Globe Democrat* reported that Commissioner Charles E. Slusser "declared himself impressed with the way that the Pruitt Homes project was being pushed into the skyline to replace a jumble of slum dwellings."[8] In 1954, the *Post-Dispatch* described the enormous Pruitt-Igoe project with its thirty-three eleven-story buildings as "bright new additions to city's skyline." The article referred to the "shabby two- and three-story row tenements that previously cluttered the site."[9] It seemed that everyone agreed that a bright and glorious future for America required erasing the old and neglected buildings from generations past. Clean, light-colored, streamlined modern skyscrapers would transform life for America's working poor.

Pruitt-Igoe opened as the individual buildings were completed in 1954 and 1955. When completed, the complex contained 2,870 low-income apartments.

The Pruitt-Igoe housing project was designed by Minoru Yamasaki, who would later design New York's World Trade Center.

This aerial view of the Pruitt-Igoe housing project in 1955 captures the scale of the complex. Each of the massive buildings measured 170 feet long. (Photo courtesy of the Missouri Historical Society)

Problems became evident almost immediately. Shortcuts in construction resulted in maintenance issues, the project lacked adequate playground space, and crime plagued the complex as soon as it was occupied.

By 1971, the huge complex housed only six hundred families, and demolition by dynamite of two of the buildings was approved in 1972. Total demolition began in 1975.

THIS USED TO BE: Pruitt-Igoe Housing Project

NOW IT'S: A Contemporary Urban Forest

LOCATION: North St. Louis

28 An Urban Forest in the Mid-Nineteenth Century

For a century before the construction of the Pruitt-Igoe housing project, its now overgrown site just northwest of downtown had been home to generations of St. Louisans.

The Irish shanty town later named Kerry Patch, begun in 1850, overlapped the site. The first settlers in the Patch, like many who would follow them, were from County Kerry. The area was woods, with only an occasional clearing, and it contained no streets or alleys. With the potato blight forcing the Irish to emigrate and many finding their way to St. Louis, the area along O'Fallon Street quickly filled with one-room, thatched-roof shanties. A big spring near 16th and O'Fallon provided water for the refugees.

By 1855, shanty Irish were working as ditch diggers, hod carriers, and teamsters. The woods had been cut away, creating a large commons area, and Cass Avenue was a plank road. Their settlement grew west to Jefferson. At first these Irish attended St. Patrick's Church to the east. In the 1850s, St. Lawrence O'Toole and St. Bridget parishes opened to serve the Irish of Kerry Patch.

In the decades following the Civil War, streets were built through Kerry Patch, and brick row houses were constructed. Beginning in the 1880s, Polish immigrants built homes side by side with the Irish, and eventually an Italian community mixed in with the Poles. In the early twentieth century, with the great migration from the South, more African Americans settled in the area.

By the turn of the century, the neighborhood's rows of narrow brick houses had white stone steps and stone lintels over the windows and

During the 1930s, neighborhood residents bought their milk from a horse-drawn milk wagon and their fruit and vegetables from an Italian street vendor who stabled his horses and delivery wagon in his backyard.

An illustration from *A Tour of St. Louis; or, the Inside Life of a Great City*, published in 1878, depicted an impoverished Kerry Patch woman in front of her shanty built of scrap material.

doors. Some houses were at the edge of the brick sidewalks, while others were set back with shallow front gardens.

Overcrowding combined with a lack of maintenance of the neighborhood houses during the Great Depression and World War II, left the neighborhood sadly neglected. Demolition to make way for modern housing projects was seen as a panacea.

THIS USED TO BE: Nineteenth-Century Ethnic Neighborhoods

NOW IT'S: An Urban Forest

LOCATION: North St. Louis

29

The Last Landmark of Kerry Patch

Though the Victorian-era palace of cherry red brick and ornamental terra-cotta at 2305 St. Louis Avenue is not within the area once called Kerry Patch, it is the only remaining landmark associated with St. Louis's historic Irish settlement. The elegant manse was the home of the last king of Kerry Patch, John J. (Jack) Sheahan.

The shanty-filled Kerry Patch was directly south of Sheahan's St. Louis Avenue mansion. Eventually, the Patch stretched from about 16th Street to Jefferson Avenue and Carr Street north to Cass Avenue. In 1855, the Patch's one-room shanties were crowded with struggling Irish immigrants.

These immigrants, mostly from County Kerry, bestowed the title "King of Kerry Patch" on Dennis Sheahan. When he passed away in 1865, his son Jack was too young for the honorary title. A man from County Cork, James Cullinane, was elected king. Years later, old residents of Kerry Patch recalled, "It was generally agreed that nobody except a Kerry man could rightfully inherit the throne. While 'king' Cullinane occupied the throne, young Jack Sheahan [reached the age of twenty-one years and there was] a big stir in the patch and a general rally of County Kerry men and their friends. A mass meeting of all the residents was called. . . . King Cullinane was deposed and young Sheahan was enthroned. The occasion was made memorable by an immense torchlight procession and a celebration that continued for several days. . . ."

The Sheahan family profited during the 1860s from nearby quarries. Jack Sheahan was a member of the police department and later formed Harrigan and Sheahan Livery and Undertaking Company with Chief of Police Lawrence Harrigan. He also served as a member of the police

As a police commissioner, Sheahan arranged that the liquor confiscated from unruly saloons be donated to homes for the aged. The free liquor was called a "godsend" for the residents.

The forgotten mansion of the influential and kindhearted Jack Sheahan. On November 15, 1935, the *St. Louis Star-Times* reporting Sheahan's death stated that he "grew up among people who knew what distress was. And this environment gave to the freckle-faced, genial boy . . . a background that carried through life with an honest regard for the Golden Rule." (Photo by Emma Prince)

The terra-cotta cartouche over the doorway gives the date the house was built, 1892 AD. (Photo by Emma Prince)

board and was serving on the St. Louis Public School Board when he and his twin brother, Patrick, built the home at the corner of St. Louis Avenue and 23rd Street. The estimated cost of construction for the impressive residence was $12,000.

THIS USED TO BE: The Sheahan Mansion

NOW IT'S: The Last Landmark of Kerry Patch

LOCATION: 2305 St. Louis Avenue

30

George B. Vashon African American Museum

Yellowed photos of African Americans in Victorian dress are displayed in the parlors of the Gilded Age town house on St. Louis Avenue that serves as the George B. Vashon African American Museum. Early twentieth-century photos in ornate oval frames show young African American men wearing the uniform of the World War I doughboy. Displays tell the stories of turn-of-the-century African American teachers, nurses, doctors, scientists, and the porters' union (the first African American union). The museum features some remarkable artifacts documenting African American history nationally, but it focuses primarily on African Americans in St. Louis and the story of that community, rooted in slavery and fighting its way to becoming a middle-class community. The stone-faced townhome that houses the museum reflects the rise from poverty of another ethnic group, the famine Irish.

Irishman James Meagher built the elegant, Second Empire townhome in 1888. Its smooth stone facade has a third-story mansard roof with an ornate cornice. Behind its recessed doorway, the hallway, parlors, and dining room feature fourteen-foot ceilings with plaster medallions, marble mantles, and elaborately milled woodwork.

Meagher, whose business career began as a grocery clerk for another Irishman, eventually owned and managed a pork packing plant on North 13th Street. The successful pork packer was a prominent member of the Merchants Exchange. When he died in his St. Louis Avenue home in 1899, his estate was valued at one million dollars.

Later, the magnificent home was converted into the Henry Leidner Funeral Home. In 1921, the undertaking company added a chapel facing St. Louis Avenue, which is clad in ornate, white, glazed terra-cotta.

A real estate ad in the *Post-Dispatch* on July 3, 1910, described the Meagher home at 2223 St. Louis Avenue: "12 rooms, bath, steam heat; fine brick stable; lot 88x144; one of the finest houses in North St. Louis."

Eastlake style details on the Meagher town house that has been converted into the George B. Vashon African American Museum. (Photo by NiNi Harris)

Museum founder Calvin Riley transformed that chapel into an exhibit room showcasing artifacts from African American history in St. Louis.

THIS USED TO BE: An Irish Immigrant's Town House

NOW IT'S: George B. Vashon African American Museum

LOCATION: 2223 St. Louis Avenue

31 A Polish Reflection

For almost 90 years, the three-story stone-faced hall on St. Louis Avenue at 20th Street regularly pulsated with vibrant polka music. The music reflected the energetic Polish American community that once surrounded the hall.

The Polish Falcons Hall, however, had an even earlier life. It was built as a private mansion by German immigrant and North City brewer Charles Stifel.

Stifel's rags to riches story began in America with him working as a farm laborer for thirteen cents a day. After many struggles, he became proprietor of the profitable City Brewery in North St. Louis. Following his service for the Union in the Civil War, Stifel's wealth grew, and he built the St. Louis Avenue mansion. With granite steps, polished granite pillars, and a slate-covered mansard roof, the mansion cost an impressive $20,000 in 1880.

Charles Stifel's son Otto continued in the brewing business until 1919, when Prohibition erased the entire brewing industry. Saddled with debt, Otto Stifel committed suicide.

In 1931, a Polish fraternal organization bought the house and its brick-walled grounds. The Polish Falcons, dedicated to a healthy spirit in a healthy body, conducted gymnastic classes and held dances in the mansion. When a fire destroyed its original roofline, the Polish Falcons quickly rebuilt the mansion, reconfiguring the upper floors as a combination gym, dance hall, and theater. In that hall, the Falcons hosted young men from Scott Air Force Base for dances during World War II. When the neighborhood boys finally returned from the war, romances began at sing-alongs around the hall's upright piano.

The Polish Falcons of America is the direct outgrowth of a similar organization that developed in Poland beginning in 1867. The St. Louis branch, or nest, was founded in 1905.

The mansion at 2013 St. Louis Avenue was home to brewer Charles Stifel, his wife, their son Otto and his wife, and Otto's in-laws. The Polish Falcons bought the house and converted it into their hall in 1931. (Courtesy of the Missouri Historical Society)

A carved granite fence post and carved granite marking the steps leading to the Polish Falcons Hall. (Photos by NiNi Harris)

The Polish community was still rejoicing and rebuilding following years of economic depression and war, when much of the Polish American neighborhood was taken by eminent domain for the construction of the Pruitt-Igoe housing project. The destruction of the core of that neighborhood began the Polish diaspora in St. Louis. Sixty-five years after the erasing of the heart of the Polish neighborhood, the Polish Falcons sold their historic hall on St. Louis Avenue in 2019.

THIS USED TO BE: A German Immigrant's Mansion

NOW IT'S: A Reflection of a Polish Neighborhood

LOCATION: 2013 St. Louis Avenue

A Storage Building

The words "Municipal Bathhouse No. 6" are written in the terra-cotta over the entrance of the one-story building on St. Louis Avenue at 11th Street that has been used for storage and workshops in recent decades. The scattering of renovated ninteenth-century homes, new homes, and extensive rain gardens disguise the fact that the surrounding Old North St. Louis neighborhood was once densely populated and that the bathhouse was built to improve health and sanitation in the then overcrowded neighborhood.

The St. Louis Avenue Bathhouse opened in 1937. The last of the municipal bathhouses constructed by the city of St. Louis, it is the only bathhouse building remaining.

The initial ordinance authorizing city bathhouses was passed in 1902, when waves of migrants from the South and immigrants from Europe were settling in the old districts along the riverfront near downtown. Most of the housing in these areas was built before modern plumbing. Residents had to use outhouses and pumps for water.

When the first bathhouses opened, one on the near north side and one on the near south side, attendance immediately numbered tens of thousands per year. By 1910, combined attendance at these two bathhouses reached a half million. Eventually, the city opened six municipal bathhouses.

The Art Deco bathhouse on St. Louis Avenue was operating in time to help with the housing crisis during World War II, when thousands more migrated from rural areas to work in St. Louis's war plants. Many workers renting a single room did not have access to a bath. For the year ending April 1943, attendance at the municipal bathhouses surpassed 780,000.

During World War II, residents taking advantage of the free showers at the municipal bathhouses had the option of buying a cake of soap for one cent and renting a towel for two cents.

Municipal Bath House No. 6 was designed by St. Louis building commissioner Albert Osburg, the architect of Homer G. Phillips Hospital. (Photo by Emma Prince)

THIS USED TO BE: Municipal Bathhouse No. 6

NOW IT'S: A Storage Building

LOCATION: 1118 St. Louis Avenue

33 Senior Apartments in the Ville Neighborhood

In the heart of North City, a seven-story work of Art Deco architecture houses 220 senior apartments. The one- and two-bedroom units fill the wings of the buff-colored brick Homer G. Phillips Senior Apartments. The complex occupies six acres at Whittier Street and St. Ferdinand Avenue in the historic African American neighborhood known as the Ville.

This apartment complex for seniors was originally built as the Homer G. Phillips Hospital for Colored in 1937. It replaced City Hospital No. 2, a 170-bed health-care center for African Americans that was dingy, overcrowded, and could not meet the needs of St. Louis's growing African American community.

The dedication of the new Homer G. Phillips Hospital was celebrated with a parade that included two thousand participants. Five thousand citizens attended the dedication ceremonies. Even President Roosevelt's secretary of the interior, Harold L. Ickes, took part in the celebration. The $3,160,000 hospital, financed with a city bond issue and PWA funds, was described by the *Post-Dispatch* as the "finest hospital of its kind for Negroes in the world."

With a capacity of 669 beds, Homer G. Phillips greatly enhanced health care for African Americans in St. Louis, but its influence was even more significant. The hospital was staffed by African American doctors, nurses, and technicians, and it also trained them, growing St. Louis's African American middle class and professional community. In 1962, the hospital administration could boast having trained more doctors and nurses of African ancestry than any other institution in the world. Over community protests, the famous city-operated hospital was closed in 1979.

A postcard image of Homer G. Phillips Hospital. (Postcard from a private collection)

City architect Albert Osburg designed the complex, with bands of terra-cotta featuring geometric designs decorating its brick walls. Osburg also designed the Soulard Market building in 1929.

THIS USED TO BE: Homer G. Phillips Hospital for Colored

NOW IT'S: Senior Apartments in the Ville Neighborhood

LOCATION: 2601 Whittier Street

Fort Belle Fontaine Park

The 306-acre Fort Belle Fontaine Park, which surrounds and includes a state-run children's home, boasts sweeping views of the Missouri River. This park that also offers intimate glens and inviting woods was the site of an Indian trading post operating at Fort Belle Fontaine, the first US military post west of the Mississippi River.

After the Louisiana Purchase, Fort Belle Fontaine was established on the Missouri River at the mouth of Coldwater Creek. As governor of the Indiana Territory, General William Harrison was given jurisdiction over the newly acquired Upper Louisiana Territory, including the fort. He signed a treaty with the Missouri Sac and Fox Indians that promised a trading post or "factory" where the Native Americans could purchase goods at a reasonable price. From 1805 to the summer of 1808, the factory operated at the fort on a narrow stretch of dry ground along the river. The factory store, which measured thirty-seven by twenty-five feet, was constructed of hand-hewn logs on a stone foundation.

The site of the trading post was not liked by the Native Americans or the European settlers. Tribes disliked the location because it was too far to carry their furs and then lug their manufactured goods back upriver. The European American settlers felt uneasy with the numbers of Native Americans arriving to trade. William Clark, residing in St. Louis, was the Indian agent for the region and advised that the trading post at Fort Belle Fontaine be closed.

The short-lived trading post was replaced by two new trading posts established at Forts Madison on the Mississippi River and Osage on the Missouri River. The military post at Fort Belle Fontaine continued operation until 1826, when it was replaced by Jefferson Barracks, located on the bluffs above the Mississippi River south of St. Louis.

A portrait of George Sibley, who served as the assistant agent at the Indian trading post at Fort Belle Fontaine. (Courtesy of the Missouri Historical Society)

THIS USED TO BE: An Indian Trading Post

NOW IT'S: Fort Belle Fontaine Park

LOCATION: 13002 Bellefontaine Road, Spanish Lake

35 Bellefontaine Road

Mid-century modern subdivisions radiate from Bellefontaine Road, a collector road frozen in the 1950s that began as a frontier trail. Baby Boomers grew up in the nearby ranch houses built by the World War II generation. Their large lots, rolling or wooded, recall the suburban dream of post–World War II America. Strip malls from the 1950s, '60s, and '70s line the rolling curbs at the major intersections of Bellefontaine Road, attesting to the role of the automobile in these suburban communities.

This suburban collector road, one of the earliest county roads in the state of Missouri, grew with the Louisiana Purchase and the arrival of early Americans. It connected early St. Louis with Fort Belle Fontaine, the military post established on the Missouri River banks in 1805 (now part of Fort Belle Fontaine Park). The General Bissell House at 10225 Bellefontaine Road is one of the few sites remaining from that nineteenth-century history.

The house dates to 1819, a decade after Connecticut native Daniel Bissell assumed command of Fort Belle Fontaine. He began acquiring land along the road and building a two-story brick home with seven rooms. After owning the house for 140 years, the Bissell family gave it to St. Louis County to serve as a museum.

Bellefontaine Road rolls through Spanish Lake, an unincorporated area filled with post–World War II cul-de-sacs. A nineteenth- and early twentieth-century farming community, it was named for the "Spanish Pond" just east of the road. French Navy officer Jacques St. Vrain owned the property with the pond, where he kept from sixty to eighty head of cattle at the turn of the nineteenth century.

Bellefontaine Road cuts through Bellefontaine Neighbors, incorporated in 1950, with nearly eleven thousand residents, and through the Spanish Lake area, with a population near twenty-one thousand.

The General Bissell House as it appeared in 1875. The original stone building, later used as a kitchen, is in the rear. (Photo courtesy of the St. Louis County Parks Department)

THIS USED TO BE: A Frontier Road

NOW IT'S: Bellefontaine Road

LOCATION: North St. Louis County

St. Louis Lambert International Airport

St. Louis Lambert International Airport—which covers 4,000 acres, serves almost sixteen million passengers annually, and boasts a stunning Modernist terminal designed by Minoru Yamasaki—evolved from the 170 acres of sod fields of the St. Louis Flying Field.

Surrounded by hotels, warehouse developments, and sprawling suburbs since the mid-twentieth century, the flying field once sat in the midst of farm country. Renamed for St. Louis aviation pioneer Albert Bond Lambert in 1923, pilots and joy riders taking off from Lambert Field during the mid- and late 1920s flew over patches of fields and forests. In the distance, they saw the Missouri River spew its muddy waters into the Mississippi. They described the different colored and textured patches created by downtown St. Louis and its surrounding neighborhoods, miles away from Lambert Field.

American aviator and inventor, Charles A. Lindbergh was flying mail between St. Louis and Chicago before his nonstop flight from New York to Paris in 1927 made him an international hero. Lindbergh described Lambert Field in those days: "There are no runways, but the clay sod is good surface for any size of aircraft during summer months. In freezing weather, gusty winds and deepening ruts make operation difficult." He wrote about "erosion on its shallow slope." Robertson Aircraft Corporation provided the major commercial activity at the field. According to Lindbergh, Robertson consisted of "a little, stove-heated office, two frame warehouses for airplane and engine parts, and half of

Young Benny Baudissin and his friends used to bicycle from their homes in South City to Lambert Field to watch the barnstorming pilots in the 1920s. Eventually Baudissin saved up the five dollar fee required to take a ride in one of the sputtering, open-cockpit planes.

A portrait of a young Charles Lindbergh, who flew air mail into St. Louis's Lambert Field. (Postcard from a private collection)

St. Louis Flying Field as it appeared in 1920. (Courtesy of the Missouri Historical Society)

When the modern, three-domed terminal at Lambert Airport was completed in 1956, it was dubbed the "Grand Central of the Air." A fourth dome was added to the terminal in 1965, which inspired other modern airport design. (Postcard from a private collection)

a civilian hangar house." The corporation reconditioned and sold army training planes and engines for what Lindbergh said were "extraordinarily low prices."[10]

During the 1920s, the airport that today has 270 daily departures had minimal activity. Lindbergh wrote that, except on weekends when the National Guard squadron was there, "there are seldom more than a half-dozen pilots on the field, and the chief activity consists of training students."[11]

THIS USED TO BE: St. Louis Flying Field
NOW IT'S: St. Louis Lambert International Airport
LOCATION: North St. Louis County

37

Urshan College

On high ground along North County's Howdershell Road, a scattering of trees and large dorms that date to the 1940s hide the nineteenth-century brick and stone buildings at the core of Urshan College. Before the college operated by the United Pentecostal Church acquired the property, Roman Catholic Jesuit priests and brothers operated these buildings and the surrounding acreage like a self-sufficient medieval monastery in Europe. The remarkable men who lived and trained in this introverted setting changed the face of frontier America, and the institutions they established continue to influence life in the American heartland.

Beginning in 1823, this was the site of St. Stanislaus Jesuit Seminary, established by Jesuit priests and seminarians from Belgium. The seminary began with a log cabin and farm. Like any pioneers, the Jesuits lived off the land. They tended an orchard and wheat crops. They raised chickens and dairy cattle and operated their own bakery and dairy. In the 1840s, they crafted the three-story limestone seminary building, and in the 1870s they began constructing brick buildings. At the same time, the Jesuit seminarians maintained a rigorous scholastic program studying theology, philosophy, the classics, Greek, and Latin. They learned the ancient arts of decorating manuscripts.

Meanwhile, the Jesuits of St. Stanislaus staffed Saint Louis University and established parishes among the newly arrived German immigrants settling along the Missouri River. Jesuit Father Pierre-Jean DeSmet, a founder of St. Stanislaus Seminary, began what would become almost annual trips to work among the Indians of the American northwest. Having earned their trust, he negotiated on behalf of the tribes with the United States government.

Jesuits trained at St. Stanislaus opened the University of Detroit, Xavier University in Cincinnati, Loyola University in Chicago, Marquette University in Milwaukee, and Creighton University in Omaha.

One of the founders of St. Stanislaus Seminary, Belgian-born Jesuit Pierre-Jean DeSmet, with Native American leaders. (Photo courtesy of the Archives of Saint Louis University's Pius XII Memorial Library)

The stone seminary building constructed by the Jesuit priests and brothers in the 1840s. (Photo courtesy of the Archives of Saint Louis University's Pius XII Memorial Library)

The seminary continued to thrive during the early twentieth century. By the time the seminary closed in 1971, approximately three thousand Jesuit seminarians had trained at St. Stanislaus. That year the seminary complex was sold to the United Pentecostal Church.

THIS USED TO BE: A Medieval-Style Seminary

NOW IT'S: Urshan College

LOCATION: 700 Howdershell Road

4500–4600 Block of Westminster Place

The apartment building at 4633 Westminster Place frames the corner of a block of beautifully crafted stone and brick, two- and three-story houses from the turn of the century. The castle-like white stone Second Presbyterian Church and the dignified brick and stucco building constructed in 1908 as the home of the prominent Wednesday Club frame the east end of the block. This gracious block was the setting for the childhood of Thomas Lanier Williams, who would grow up to be the great American playwright Tennessee Williams.

The elegant entrance to the apartment building at 4629–33 Westminster Place. (Photo by Brian Kolde)

Williams's first eight years of childhood were spent most joyously in Mississippi near his beloved maternal grandparents. In 1918, his father took a job with International Shoe in St. Louis, bringing the family to the city. C. C. Williams found an apartment in the corner building at 4633 Westminster Place for his family's first St. Louis home.

Decades later, after he had won acclaim for his plays *The Glass Menagerie*, *A Streetcar Named Desire*, and *Cat on a Hot Tin Roof* and after many of his plays had been made into movies, Tennessee Williams described that Central West End block in his *Memoirs:* "Our first home in St. Louis was on Westminster Place, a pleasant residential street lined with great trees which made it almost Southern in appearance." He recalled his and his sister Rose's childhood life on Westminster: "Rose and I made friends and we had an agreeable children's life among them, playing 'hide-and-seek' and 'fly, sheep, fly,' and bathing under garden hoses in the hot summer. We were only a block from the Lorelei swimming pool and the West End Lyric movie and we had bicycle races about the block."[12]

Fire escapes on the back of 4633 Westminster are reminiscent of the fire escape the main character sat on in Williams's classic *The Glass Menagerie*. (Photo by Brian Kolde)

In 1937, one of Tennessee Williams's earliest plays, *Fugitive Kind*, was produced at the Wednesday Club, the influential women's club at 4504 Westminster Place.

THIS USED TO BE: The Childhood Playground of Playwright Tennessee Williams

NOW IT'S: 4500–4600 Block of Westminster Place

LOCATION: Central West End

39

Chess Club and Scholastic Center of Saint Louis

The Chess Club, a mecca for chess players from around the world, fills charming storefronts on Maryland Avenue that date to 1898. The electrification of streetcar service to the neighborhood in the early 1890s had spurred the surrounding residential development and the construction of this row of storefronts on the northeast corner of Maryland and Euclid Avenues. Their cast-iron columns, garland designs in terra-cotta, and gothic arches over the doorways to the second-floor apartments, which now house tournament rooms, give these storefronts elegance.

At the beginning of the twentieth century, local businesses in these storefronts catered to the city's social and entrepreneurial elite who lived in the nearby private places. In 1909, the Mercantile Grocery Co. was located in the site of the Chess Club. While storefronts in the neighborhoods of factory workers housed shoe repair businesses, dry goods stores, and poultry shops, some of the Maryland Avenue businesses supplied comparative luxuries. The Maryland Floral Company filled the site of the Kingside Diner (a diner that carries chess matches on televisions like sports bars carry football games). A hatmaker, a dressmaker, and Leon Rovitsky's tailor shop occupied other storefronts in the row.

Since 2008, the Chess Club and Scholastic Center, dedicated to promoting this old and beloved game, has hosted the world's greatest players in these historic storefronts. It has a tournament hall and a broadcast center in addition to tables set up for pickup games. Along the tree-shaded sidewalk outside the Chess Club, chess players from near and far gather around cafe tables topped with terrazzo chess boards for pickup games.

Yiddish-speaking tailor Leon Rovitsky was born in Russia about 1865. He immigrated to America as a young man and eventually became a naturalized United States citizen.

Elaborate terra-cotta frames the windows and doors of the Chess Club's building. (Photo by Brian Kolde)

THIS USED TO BE: Neighborhood Businesses for the Elite

NOW IT'S: Chess Club and Scholastic Center of Saint Louis

LOCATION: 4657 Maryland Avenue

40

Maryland Plaza

Seven stately mansions atop terraces face Maryland Plaza. The impressive buildings, redeveloped as twenty elegant townhomes, share a block-long front garden surrounded by handsome iron fencing. A line of new carriage houses on Carriage House Lane, with balconies that double as trellises for wisteria, is tucked behind the fashionable townhomes. This extraordinary redevelopment of the historic place adds new layers of charm to century-old Maryland Plaza.

Originally a private place, Maryland Plaza's mansions were home to wealthy and socially prominent St. Louisans whose names regularly appeared in the social register. The 1910 census recorded seven households in the row of then new mansions that were built in 1905 and 1906. The heads of households included three physicians, a lumber merchant, and a newspaper editor.

Found in the census (but not mentioned in the social register) were the servants who lived in the three-story mansions. They scrubbed the laundry, peeled the potatoes, and beat the carpets for their aristocratic employers. The family of Dr. George Tuttle, son of the Episcopal bishop, had two live-in servants. Sidney B. Thayer and his wife and daughter, who lived off their investments, had a housekeeper, a maid, and a cook. Eugenia Chouteau and her niece had three live-in servants. Dr. Greenfield Sluder and his family had a cook, two nurses, and two maids. The live-in servants recorded at the seven mansions totaled twenty-one. Their ethnic backgrounds did not reflect the ethnic mix of the general population of St. Louis in 1910. Nine of the servants were born in America. One was an immigrant from England, two were immigrants from Scotland, and nine were Irish-born Americans.

THIS USED TO BE: The Home of Servants and Saks Fifth Avenue

NOW IT'S: Maryland Plaza

LOCATION: Central West End

When Saks Fifth Avenue and Montaldo's occupied the commercial buildings on Maryland Plaza, chauffeured limousines used to line up on Maryland Plaza to let ladies off at the doors. (Photo by Brian Kolde)

Century-old mansions atop terraces behind the deep lawns on Maryland Avenue. (Photo by Brian Kolde)

During the 1930s, stylish Art Deco–inspired, yellow brick and black vitrolite commercial buildings were constructed on the south side of Maryland Plaza, opposite the mansions. By 1956, Saks Fifth Avenue and the exclusive Montaldo's stores filled these glamorous edifices.

2 Hortense Place

Stone and iron gates mark the Euclid Avenue entrance to prestigious Hortense Place in the city's Central West End. The impressive home of the man who made a fortune in Listerine and was nicknamed the Dean of Aviation in St. Louis can be seen through these imposing gates. The design of Lambert's red-brick mansion, shaded by the street's giant trees, is symmetrical and dignified. A two-story rounded portico supported by columns with Corinthian capitals shelters the main entrance.

Walking up the steps to the double doors of this great house must have been intimidating to young, shy aviator Charles Lindbergh. In 1926, Lindbergh went there seeking financial support from Lambert for his proposed transatlantic flight in a single-engine plane. Not only did Lambert immediately offer financial support, but he encouraged others to underwrite the endeavor. In their honor, the plane that was financed by Lambert and his friends and carried Lindbergh on his historic flight was named *The Spirit of St. Louis*.

Albert Bond Lambert had made his fortune through an extremely successful pharmaceutical company founded by his father. His love, however, was every aspect of air travel. At the beginning of the century, he secured numerous balloon races for St. Louis. In 1910, he qualified as a licensed pilot. (Orville Wright was one of his flight instructors.) As a commissioned officer in the US Army during World War I, he directed the training of pilots.

St. Louis Lambert International Airport began when Albert Bond Lambert converted a North County cornfield into a flying field. Lambert's constant support made St. Louis preeminent in aeronautics.

In 1923, the city's first international air races were at the field that Lambert converted into a "flying field," now St. Louis Lambert International Airport.

The imposing home of Albert Bond Lambert. (Photo by Brian Kolde)

In his portraits, aviation pioneer Albert Bond Lambert appears a mild-mannered executive. His pharmaceutical company prospered manufacturing Listerine. (Photo courtesy of the Missouri Historical Society)

THIS USED TO BE: Home of Aviation Pioneer Albert Bond Lambert

NOW IT'S: 2 Hortense Place

LOCATION: Central West End

Dorris Loft Condominiums

In the mid-1980s, the conversion of an old auto factory into the Dorris Loft Condominiums showed the way to save St. Louis's wealth of historic buildings. The transformation of the three-story industrial building of reinforced concrete sheathed in brick was described as "the first loft condominium development in the St. Louis area."[13]

The condominium building was constructed in 1911–1912 as the plant and showroom for one of St. Louis's early innovative carmakers—George Dorris. He had worked with the St. Louis Motor Carriage Company, begun in 1898. When the other men involved in that company decided to move their plant to Peoria, Illinois, Dorris stayed in St. Louis and started his own company. The Dorris Company produced its first car in 1906—a high-end, handcrafted car called "the Dorris." The slogans—"The Silent Car," "Built up to a standard, not down to price," "Built to Last," and "Ask the Man Who Owns One"—made the car desirable despite its substantial price tag. In 1914, Dorris's cars cost about $2,500, the cost of a small, well-built brick home.

The banks of windows fill the Dorris Lofts with abundant natural light. (Photo by Brian Kolde)

While Henry Ford was experimenting with assembly line production and reducing costs, Dorris maintained his quality. Rather than try to be competitive

At the beginning of the twentieth century, ten St. Louis–based automakers were turning out four million dollars in cars annually.

A 1919 model Dorris automobile manufactured in the Laclede Avenue factory. (Photo courtesy of the Missouri Historical Society)

with the cheaper assembly line autos, George Dorris closed his car company in 1926. He had crafted three thousand vehicles.

The auto plant and showroom had two more lives before it was converted into thirty-nine residential lofts. Beginning in 1928, Cadillac dealers occupied the building. Then the army requisitioned the Dorris factory building during World War II to house the McDonnell Aircraft engineering department and model shop.

THIS USED TO BE: An Automobile Factory

NOW IT'S: Dorris Loft Condominiums

LOCATION: 4100 Laclede Avenue

Evangeline's Bistro

The restaurant and cafe building at the busy corner of Euclid and Washington Avenue, with its stuccoed walls and red-tile roofs, looks like a bit of old Hollywood during the era of the silent movies. Evangeline's Bistro occupies this corner building that features an interior with dark-stained wood piers and beams. This luxurious environment was originally designed as a showroom for the glamorous Pierce-Arrow automobiles. The building's expansive windows showcased the cars to passersby.

The successful Pierce-Arrow dealer, ambitious Sam Breadon, went on to own the St. Louis Cardinals.

Sam Breadon guided the St. Louis Cardinals to six World Series titles. (Photo Courtesy of the Missouri Historical Society)

The son of Irish immigrants, Breadon grew up in New York near the docks. His Horatio Alger story began when he followed friends to St. Louis. He was down to living on fifteen cents a day when he talked himself into a stake in a popcorn stand at the World's Fair. With money he made from the concession at the Fair, he opened up a garage. By 1917, Breadon was part owner of the Pierce-Arrow dealership. Meanwhile, he had bought into the struggling St. Louis Cardinals with an initial investment of two hundred dollars. By 1919, he was president of the Cardinals and soon owned a 51 percent interest in the team.

Breadon was known as a quiet man of few words, except when it came to gathering around a piano with his old cronies and singing favorite Irish songs.

Breadon's two hundred dollar investment in the St. Louis Cardinals grew into a three million dollar asset.

The sidewalk cafe of Evangeline's Bistro. (Photo by Brian Kolde)

As owner of the Cardinals, he was considered a remarkable operator. A *Saturday Evening Post* article described Breadon's methods: "He sells off his St. Louis Cardinal stars, second-guesses his managers, but keeps winning the pennants and pulling in the cash."[14] During Sam Breadon's twenty-seven-year ownership and leadership, the St. Louis Cardinals developed a minor league farm system and won nine pennants and six World Series titles.

THIS USED TO BE: Pierce-Arrow Dealership That Paid for the Cardinals

NOW IT'S: Evangeline's Bistro

LOCATION: 512 North Euclid

Forest Park (The Southeastern Corner)

Thirteen-hundred-acre Forest Park is the nation's stellar urban park. Its natural areas include prairie, savanna, and forest. Its formal areas feature fountains, lagoons, and grand vistas. It is home to the region's great cultural institutions.

This phenomenal urban park sweetened life during the most threatening of times for St. Louisans and for all Americans. During the Great Depression, the park and its free attractions became "St. Louis's greatest playground."[15] Later, after the Japanese attack on Pearl Harbor thrust the United States into the deadliest war in history, the park's southeastern corner gave comfort and distraction to young soldiers as an army recreational camp.

In the early part of July 1942, the United States Army was granted permission to use a seventeen-acre tract in the southeastern corner of Forest Park for the duration of the war. On that tract, the army developed a recreational camp with huts that could accommodate fifteen hundred men. When these young soldiers, many away from home for the first time, received a weekend leave, they could spend it at the camp in Forest Park. It was described as "the finest camp that the Army is operating anywhere in this country."[16] Without a nickel spent on carfare, the soldiers could enjoy the soccer or baseball fields, visit the zoo or the art museum, or see a musical at the Municipal Opera.

By 1947, the recreational camp was no longer needed, and the army began removing the huts. The St. Louis Parks and Recreation Department annual report of 1948 noted that the site had been restored, erasing all signs that young men burdened with defeating the Axis had found respite there.

In 1941, the Jewel Box attracted nearly a half million visitors with its seasonal shows.

A supply tent at the Army Recreational Camp that operated in Forest Park during World War II. (Photo courtesy of the Missouri Historical Society)

THIS USED TO BE: An Army Recreational Camp

NOW IT'S: Forest Park (The Southeastern Corner)

LOCATION: Central West End

Missouri Historical Society Library and Research Center

The streamlined variation of Istanbul's domed Hagia Sophia that faces Forest Park serves as the bank for St. Louis's most precious valuables—the fragile journals, the rare tomes, and the yellowed photos of our civic ancestors. As the Library and Research Center of the Missouri Historical Society, this early twentieth-century building inspired by the sixth-century Turkish cathedral is the storehouse for the documents that reveal our shared history.

Opening the doors of its three-story entrance bay, with banks of windows above the doors forming a huge Roman arch, is an awe-inspiring experience. Inside, the vestibule opens into the reading room, capped by a forty-foot dome. Gold highlights illuminate the lush, richly colored, ornate plastered ceiling.

This extraordinary environment was created for a sacred use. It was built as the United Hebrew Temple and dedicated in 1927. The congregation was the first Jewish congregation established west of the Mississippi River. With 650 member families, United Hebrew was also the largest Jewish group in the city when the congregation built its temple on Skinker.

The domed reading room was the sanctuary. Opening the velvet curtains that closed off the side wings added seating for 750 more members. The seating for the sanctuary, balconies, and side wings

When the United Hebrew congregation bought the property on Skinker for its new spiritual home, some nearby residents objected and sued. Litigation went all the way to the Missouri Supreme Court, which dismissed the lawsuit.

The interior of the Missouri Historical Society's Library and Research Center when it was home to the oldest Jewish congregation west of the Mississippi. (Courtesy of the Missouri Historical Society)

added up to 2,200. St. Louis architecture firm of Maritz & Young with Gabriel Ferrand designed the temple that was the home of the United Hebrew congregation for more than sixty years.

In 1992, the United Hebrew Temple was converted into the Library and Research Center of the Missouri Historical Society.

THIS USED TO BE: United Hebrew Temple

NOW IT'S: Missouri History Museum Library and Research Center

LOCATION: 225 South Skinker

City Hall of University City

The city hall of University City—a five-story octagon topped by a dome—is a one-of-a-kind structure. Its terra-cotta ornament featuring brackets, cartouches, garlands, and flowery designs is so extravagant that the building looks like a cake with excessive icing decoration. This remarkable city hall has ninety-seven thousand square feet of office space and meeting rooms.

The city hall was built as the executive office building of entrepreneur Edward G. Lewis, who had mastered the pyramid scheme. Lewis, the Yankee descendant of Episcopal clergymen, could sell patent medicines and Anti-Skeet (a mosquito repellent very popular in St. Louis) with the inspiration and verve of a preacher. Seeing the possibilities in publishing, he bought an inexpensive magazine, *The Winner*, with a printing office in downtown St. Louis.

In 1902, Lewis changed the name of the publication to the *Woman's Magazine*. Rural women from across the nation sold subscriptions to the *Woman's Magazine* with the promise that their sales would fund the building of women's clubhouses in their counties or small towns. (Some did get built.) With this advertising base, he haphazardly created, promoted, and sold diverse business interests that sounded like noble and egalitarian endeavors—the American Women's League, the People's Bank, the People's University, and even University City real estate. Meanwhile, Lewis served as mayor of University City.

He chose the highest ground in his University City property to build his executive office building in 1903. Known as the "Magazine Building," it stood 135 feet high.

A furniture storage company was renting part of the Magazine Building and the rest was empty when University City mayor Eugene Ruth acquired it in 1930 to serve as the University City City Hall.

University City's octagonal city hall was identified as E. G. Lewis's "Woman's Magazine Building" on this postcard. (Postcard from a private collection)

By 1911, Lewis's chaotic and underfinanced empire was disintegrating. On June 26, 1912, his buildings and equipment were auctioned at a receiver's sale. He packed a train with furnishings, including the chandelier from the Magazine Building's lobby, and headed for California.

THIS USED TO BE: The Magazine Building

NOW IT'S: City Hall of University City

LOCATION: 6801 Delmar Boulevard

47 A Clayton Neighborhood

Wydown Boulevard leads to the core of a charming, early twentieth-century residential enclave surrounded by Clayton's booming commerce. Polo Drive winds and gently turns through the rolling and shaded landscape of this enclave named Country Club Place. Along the drive, large, comfortable homes—some built of dark textured brick, some with steeply pitched slate roofs, and some with stuccoed walls—date to the 1920s and 1930s.

At the turn of the century, Wydown Boulevard led to the old St. Louis Country Club. Where Polo Drive loops through the landscape, the club was headquartered in a gracious, Colonial-style, frame clubhouse. The rambling clubhouse, with dining facilities, lounges, balconies, and shady porches, was the focal point of the club's thirty-four acres in Clayton. Club members apparently leased additional land from the surrounding Davis estate for their golf course, the current site of Davis Drive.

The club was established in 1892 as the area's first country club. Its membership numbered 15. By 1895, its membership had grown to 25 perpetual and 250 regular members. That year the club moved from its original home on a Bridgeton farm to its acreage at the center of Clayton. With its ranks filling with descendants of old St. Louis families and executives of major companies, the club was earning the reputation of being "the millionaires' paradise."

On January 1, 1912, the club membership voted to sell the Clayton property and buy new land farther west. They purchased a 227-acre tract in Ladue from the St. Louis Archdiocese. In 1914, the club's Clayton acreage was developed as Country Club Place.

The archbishop used the money from the sale of the Ladue property to the St. Louis Country Club to buy the tract southwest of St. Louis where Kenrick Seminary was developed.

This postcard, showing the old clubhouse of the St. Louis Country Club in Clayton, was printed between 1907 and 1912. (Postcard from a private collection)

THIS USED TO BE: St. Louis Country Club

NOW IT'S: A Clayton Neighborhood

LOCATION: West St. Louis

Suburban St. Louis County

Almost a million people call St. Louis County home. Their houses, apartments, big-box stores, offices, and schools fill the county's 523 square miles. Their ranch homes circle cul-de-sacs radiating from collector roads. Strip malls line their major roads.

Some major county roads wander because they began as country roads that followed ridges or creek beds. More of these suburban collector roads—Gravois, Olive, Manchester—radiate from the city like spokes on a wheel because they evolved as farm-to-market roads.

The patterns of the major roads can be traced to the county's recent past as a cornucopia overflowing with produce that fed city residents—strawberries and cantaloupes that were sweet as candy, juicy peaches, tasty corn, and peppers so abundant that in September the smell of stuffed green peppers radiated from kitchen windows all over South City. In fall, city housewives bought beets by the bushel from county farmers, simmered them with cinnamon sticks, and canned them to enjoy all winter long. Since county farmers provided generations of their city neighbors with a wealth of produce ripened in the fields, it's not surprising that the old official seal of St. Louis County showed a plow breaking earth.

At the turn of the century, when the population of St. Louis County numbered only fifty thousand, its farms enveloped towns like Florissant, Manchester, Kirkwood, Ferguson, and Clayton, the county seat.

Though the county's population had ballooned to over 274,000 by 1940, the census described 2,743 citizens of St. Louis County as farmers or farm managers. These numbers reflected thousands of acres of farmland.

In the 1960s, county farmers still drove the city's streets hawking fruits and vegetables from the backs of their pick-up trucks.

The St. Louis County seal, adopted in 1876, depicts a farmer's plow.

In the 1950s, "a ride in the country" still meant a ride along Gravois, Bellefontaine Road, or Union Road and stopping at a farmer's homemade roadside stand to buy tomatoes ripened on the vine. That decade, however, witnessed suburban development stealing the rich farmland. The number of farmers and farm managers shrank during the 1950s from almost 2,000 to only 761.

THIS USED TO BE: A Cornucopia of Farm Produce

NOW IT'S: Suburban St. Louis County

LOCATION: St. Louis County

49

Leon R. Strauss Center of the Community Music School

The music of violins floats from small studio rooms through the rambling conservatory set among the pine trees of Faust Park. The stuccoed, Mission Revival conservatory features beamed ceilings, abundant leaded glass, and a massive fireplace. The exotic building, home of the Leon R. Strauss Center of the Community Music School, is suited for use as a conservatory. It was built, however, as the sprawling Southwestern-style residence of one of St. Louis's most aristocratic families.

The patriarch of the family was German immigrant and restaurateur Tony Faust. His famous Oyster House in downtown St. Louis was the talk of the Midwest and created the family's initial wealth. His son Edward became a wealthy industrialist. Edward married Anna Louise Busch, scion of the German American brewer. They built the grandest home in the Central West End, 1 Portland Place, with 18,844 square feet.

Their son Leicester Busch Faust dreamed of being a farmer and was especially interested in raising chickens. His mother, wishing "to give him an opportunity to run a farm of his own during the summer, before he enters Harvard," bought him eighty acres near the town of Chesterfield. The price tag for that acreage, the beginnings of his farm, was $20,000.[17] That was in 1917, and Leicester was only eighteen. He chose St. Louis architect Tom Barnett, who had designed his parents' mansion on Portland Place, to design his farm home to reflect the native architecture of the American Southwest. He named his farm for the ancient Pueblo symbol, Swastika Farm.

Even the chicken coops on Leicester Faust's farm were designed by noted architect Tom Barnett.

Photo showing the original entrance gate to Leicester Faust's farm with a swastika, long before Hitler turned that ancient Pueblo design into a symbol of hate. (Courtesy of St. Louis County Parks)

Half a century later, Leicester Faust and his wife, Mary, donated 98.5 acres of their farm to St. Louis County for a park. Later, a bequest from Mary Faust doubled the size of the park. In 1994, the Community Music School opened its West County center in the Faust's farmhouse, thanks to developer and philanthropist Leon R. Strauss.

THIS USED TO BE: Home of Leicester Faust on his Swastika Farm

NOW IT'S: Leon R. Strauss Center of the Community Music School

LOCATION: Faust Park

50

Frontenac Hilton Hotel

With its eye-catching eight-sided, three-story porte cochere topped by a cupola, the 263-room Frontenac Hilton Hotel is a landmark on Lindbergh Boulevard at Highway 40. It was built in 1974 with an addition in 1984. Adjacent to Le Chateau Village and near Plaza Frontenac, it is part of a ritzy lineup on Lindbergh.

During the days when Route 66 followed this stretch of Lindbergh through St. Louis County, this was the site of the Smith Brothers Motel. It was built during the era of independently operated motor courts or small motels with cabins or cottages for rent. Smith Brothers consisted mostly of two-unit brick cottages with each unit warmed by a gas heater. The motel office had a second-floor dining room.

At the end of World War II, Al Block and his partner, Les Nieman, bought the old Smith Brothers Motel and renamed it the King Brothers Motel. There were farms and woods nearby, and Route 66 led travelers into the nearby foothills of the Ozarks. The Pilot's Room Steak House operated in the second floor over the office. Block advertised that the King Brothers Motel offered twenty-four-hour telephone service, a "modern" coffee shop, a cocktail lounge, a steakhouse, "nitely" dancing, and a swimming pool. David Block, son of owner Al Block, recalled, "A guy leased the Pilot's Room and turned it into a night club and booked Hollywood acts there." Among the entertainers was vaudeville-trained comedian Morey Amsterdam, who played sidekick to Dick Van Dyke on his popular sitcom.

The motel, with sophisticated dining and entertainment in an isolated area, had an allure that attracted characters. Frank "Buster" Wortman, who controlled East Side rackets, was a regular at the steakhouse. According to David Block, Wortman "was not allowed to come over, he snuck over. I think he liked one of the waitresses."

Al Block turned down members of the crew of the television series *Route 66*, who wanted free rooms to include shots of the motel in one of its episodes.

Postcards touted the amenities of the Smith Brothers Motel, later renamed the King Brothers Motel, in a then rural area outside St. Louis. (Postcard from a private collection)

Al Block passed away in 1972, and his partner died about the same time. Their attorney sold the motel when the character of the old highway was evolving into a high-end commercial district.

THIS USED TO BE: King Brothers Motel, the Hangout of an East-Side Racketeer

NOW IT'S: Frontenac Hilton Hotel

LOCATION: West St. Louis

Maryville Centre Corporate Park

Maryville Centre Corporate Park, with its office buildings sheathed in dark reflective glass and bands of brick or polished granite, faces always busy Highway 40. Hidden behind the corporate park, but tied to its history, is the campus of Maryville University. Erased from the acreage, however, is any evidence of its history as farmland.

In 1961, the Religious of the Sacred Heart purchased the acreage between Conway Road and Interstate 40 for the new West County campus of Maryville College. The college sold the southern border of its property facing Highway 40, including a log farmhouse built by nineteenth-century settlers Ludwig and Katherine Mertz, for development as the corporate park. The log home still stood on the site while the office buildings of the corporate park rose around it.

Mertz, an immigrant from Alsace-Lorraine, had bought thirty acres in 1846 for eight hundred dollars. In steps, Ludwig and Katherine Mertz built a two-room log house with a dog trot. They raised apples, peaches, cherries, and berries and smoked meat in their own smokehouse.

When the family of Nancy Tindall Clifford rented the house and thirty acres in 1942, twentieth-century amenities had not been added. "My father rented the cabin at that time for $10 a month. . . . We burned wood for heating and cooking, used kerosene lamps for light, and our water came from a cistern outside. I can remember my mother heating water in a galvanized tub for washing and using a washboard.

"We were quite isolated at the time. We children had to walk three miles to a school called Locust Grove at Ladue and Mason. A car would only occasionally come down Highway 40."[18]

In 1986, the Mertz cabin, then next to concrete parking lots and in the shadow of new office buildings, was moved to the historic village in Faust Park.

The Ludwig and Katherine Mertz log house in its original setting on the Maryville campus. The original chinking between the logs is still visible on the end wall. (Photo courtesy of the St. Louis County Parks Department)

THIS USED TO BE: Maryville University Campus and the Mertz Farm

NOW IT'S: Maryville Centre Corporate Park

LOCATION: West St. Louis

52

Park Avenue Plaza

Ornamental grasses, walkways, and benches surround the fountain in Lafayette Square's Park Avenue Plaza. The plaza, with its fountain featuring a column topped by a Corinthian capital, is the focal point of the square's Victorian-era business district along Park Avenue.

This block of land was transformed into a delightful neighborhood centerpiece only in recent years. During the Gilded Age, the plaza was the site of car stables for the horse-drawn streetcars. When the neighborhood was declining at the turn-of-the-century, the American Bed Company built a factory adjacent to the car stables. They manufactured iron beds, cots, and wire spring mattresses in their two-story brick factory. By the mid-twentieth century, the car stables had become an auto junkyard. A ramshackle, galvanized metal fence partly enclosed the yard. Explosions occurred regularly, and the stench of burning tires often emanated from the eyesore.

After years of struggle, the city gained control of the property. Neighborhood residents working with St. Louis's Lawrence Group developed the plan for the plaza, which features drought-resistant plantings and rain gardens. Increased revenue from taxes in the immediate area financed the new plaza, which was completed in 2004.

The adjacent Western Wire Products Company factory at 1415 South 18th Street was converted into Sqwires Restaurant and loft apartments known as the WireWorks Lofts. In 2001, it opened with eighty apartments surrounding a courtyard pool.

During the Great Depression, Western Wire Works acquired the American Bed Company factory building and employed many Bohemian Americans who lived in the surrounding residences.

The tree-lined walks in the Park Avenue Plaza lead to the fountain with its massive column. The ornate capital atop the column was salvaged from an 1880s bank building. (Photo by Emma Prince)

THIS USED TO BE: A Junkyard

NOW IT'S: Park Avenue Plaza

LOCATION: Park Avenue and 18th Street

53 A Lafayette Square Victorian Town House

The elegant town house at 1024 Mississippi Avenue has features typical of Lafayette Square's Victorian-era architecture. Its tall, narrow facade is clad in smooth stone and punctuated by tall windows and ornately milled double doors. Other features, like the missing third floor and an apse added to the back of the first floor, hint that this house's story has unique twists.

Joseph Schnaider built this town house, along with others in the immediate vicinity, in 1879. The German-born brewer had operated the Schnaider Brewery on nearby Chouteau Avenue beginning in 1865. His beer garden, which covered the block opposite the town house on Mississippi, had achieved national fame. On summer evenings, thousands enjoyed the garden with its music pavilions, shade trees, flowers, and grottoes.

Unlike most Lafayette Square houses that have mansard roofs or the elaborate cornices of the Italianate style, 1024 Mississippi is only two stories tall and is topped with a gabled roof. The original third floor and roof were likely ripped off by the deadly tornado that swept through the near south side and devastated Lafayette Square on May 27, 1896.

In 1918, the Albanian Orthodox Church of St. Louis purchased the house. To transform the building into a church, the Albanians removed most of the walls on the first floor. With the parlors, dining room, and kitchen walls removed, the shallow one-story addition on the back of the former kitchen served as an apse providing a backdrop for the sanctuary. They named their church in honor of St. Dimitry.

The Albanians sold their church to a congregation of the Church of God in 1935. The town house served as a church for almost fifty years. In 1976, when an urban pioneer began restoring the building as a home, church pews still furnished the first floor.

The entrance to the Victorian home at 1024 Mississippi was once the entrance to a sanctuary. (Photo by NiNi Harris)

THIS USED TO BE: An Albanian Orthodox Church

NOW IT'S: A Lafayette Square Victorian Town House

LOCATION: 1024 Mississippi Avenue

Abbey on the Park Condominiums

The white stone Abbey on the Park condominium building facing Lafayette Park—with its steep gabled roof, Gothic-arched doorways, and lancet stained glass windows piercing its stone walls—was built as the Lafayette Square Presbyterian Church.

The church's origins date to the fall of 1875 when residents of the already glamorous Lafayette Square neighborhood organized weekly prayer meetings and Bible readings. They met at the grand home of successful businessman Edward Bredell, until their membership grew to 150. Then they purchased the parcel of ground at Missouri Avenue opposite enchanting Lafayette Park. On January 13, 1878, they held their first services in the completed ground floor of the unfinished church.

Members of the new congregation included D. C. Jaccard of the international jeweler Mermod & Jaccard and architect John H. Maurice, who had designed homes in the neighborhood. In the spring of 1881, they chose Maurice to design the upper floors of their church.

Even the annual church directories, with dark red velveteen covers featuring gold embossed lettering, reflected the congregation's early prosperity. This prosperity continued for many years, but like the neighborhood, its prestige faded over time. In 1946, the struggling congregation merged with the Presbyterian church in the Shaw neighborhood. The magnificent stone church sat vacant for years before it was renovated as nine spectacular condominiums featuring fourteen-foot ceilings and dramatic windows.

A stained glass window on the south wall of the sanctuary was dedicated to the son of Edward Bredell Sr., a Confederate volunteer who had been killed at the Battle of Fredericksburg.

Gothic arches and massive wood doors with medieval-style hinges open into the condos facing lush Lafayette Park. (Photo by Emma Prince)

THIS USED TO BE: A Presbyterian Church

NOW IT'S: Abbey on the Park Condominiums

LOCATION: 1505 Missouri Avenue

55

The Bordeaux

Long-known by Lafayette Square residents as "the mop factory," the three-and-a-half-story dark brick warehouse at Park Avenue and Dolman Street was constructed by the Zittlosen Tent and Awning Company. Established in 1867, the company produced everything that was made of canvas, including tents, tarpaulins, and camp furniture. In the days before air conditioning, Zittlosen's window awnings cooled downtown office buildings. The company even produced the canvas coverings for prairie schooners.

The company moved from its riverfront location to its new factory on Dolman in 1910. Zittlosen vice president Ernest H. Schultz was so successful that he built himself a fifteen-room residence on Longfellow Boulevard in Compton Heights, the private place that welcomed Germans.

Times were good for St. Louis German Americans like Schultz. Their influence in the city's cultural, civic, and business life was reaching new heights.

When the assassination of Archduke Franz Ferdinand of Austria triggered a series of army mobilizations and then erupted into the bloody battlefields of World War I, everything began to disintegrate for St. Louis Germans. Derogatory words like "Hun" gradually crept into American conversations about Germans. By the time the US entered the war, German Americans were demonized. Even a German name could be a source of suspicion.

When the guns of World War I were finally silenced at 11 a.m. on November 11, 1918, St. Louis's Germanic culture was forever diminished. By 1920, the name Zittlosen Manufacturing Co. had disappeared from St. Louis city directories. Instead, the nonethnic "Textile Products Mfg. Co., Tents" was listed as operating in the big warehouse at 1330 Dolman Street.

Since the 1920s, the building has been used by a number of manufacturers including Bouras Mop Manufacturing.

The ornate terra-cotta over the doorway recalls that the altered and neglected factory with boarded windows was once the impressive manufacturing operations of Zittlosen Manufacturing Company at 1332 Dolman Street. (Photo by Emma Prince)

After being used as a warehouse and factory for a variety of industries, the building called "the Mop Factory" went through a radical transformation in 2019. The factory that produced the covers for covered wagons became The Bordeaux—an apartment building with 51 trendy units and a rooftop garden offering views of the Downtown skyline.

THIS USED TO BE: Zittlosen Manufacturing, a German-American Success Story

NOW IT'S: The Bourdeaux Apartment Building

LOCATION: 1322–1332 Dolman Street

Preston Art Glass Studio

The Preston Art Glass building, with ornamental cast-iron framing its tall windows and transoms, is a lone landmark of the hardworking international community that called the 2600 and 2700 blocks of Chouteau Avenue home during the 1930s. Sprawling parking lots and low modern warehouses now surround the three-story studio building that dates to the Victorian era. Inside the studio, a couple hundred art glass windows hang from the ceiling above wood workbenches where windows are repaired or crafted. Sunlight shines through the hanging windows, showering color.

The building was constructed in stages beginning in the mid-nineteenth century. The ornate cast-iron facade appears to date to 1888, when the original building was expanded. Through the decades, a grocery store, a saloon, and later an auto company occupied the first-floor store. For nearly six decades, beginning in 1935, 2651 Chouteau housed a seed company.

At that time, old commercial buildings with second-story tenements filled the surrounding street. In 1930, Russian immigrants living on the 2600 and 2700 blocks of Chouteau found work as a grocer, a dry goods merchant, a tailor, and a junk dealer. African Americans who had moved to St. Louis from Texas, Kentucky, Mississippi, and Alabama lived on the blocks. They worked in the stockyards, as maids, as a laundress, and as a porter. Residents included the son of Italian immigrants who managed a cigar store. The Serbians and Croatians on the street found work as laborers in a stone quarry, a glass factory, and a battery factory.

During the 1930s, the Slavic surnames of the residents and small businessmen near the Preston Art Glass building included Glogovac, Bosodin, Marichich, Zoricic, Kriskovic, Mikecin, Petkovich, Sokolic, Svaglic, Matycich, Vlastelic, Lauzaich, and Anzulovich.

The studio and warehouse of Preston Art Glass as it appeared ca. 1890 when it was Henry Edler's grocery store. (Photo courtesy of the Missouri Historical Society)

Rents for most of the apartments ranged from $12.50 to $30 per month. Only three families, German Americans from an earlier generation of immigrants, owned the buildings they lived in.

THIS USED TO BE: A Grocery Store, a Saloon, and Atlas Seed Company

NOW IT'S: Preston Art Glass Studio

LOCATION: 2651 Chouteau Avenue

Turnverein Condominiums

An ornamental iron gate opens into the courtyard of the Turnverein Condominiums in the LaSalle Park neighborhood of South St. Louis. Thirty-six units surround the three-level courtyard with its stone-walled sunken room and second-story wood walkways. When the condominiums were developed in 1981, the building was already a century old.

It was built in stages in 1881, 1884, and 1905 as the home of the South St. Louis Turnverein, a German gymnastic association. Within these walls, German Americans studied and practiced gymnastics as developed by the father of modern gymnastics, Friedrich Ludwig Jahn. They exercised with dumbbells, vaulted onto pommel horses, walked on balance beams, and swung on rings suspended from the ceilings.

These Turner clubs had a political, cultural, and social character. They encouraged physical fitness as part of public education and supported improved working conditions. The South St. Louis Turnverein encouraged an active social environment by sponsoring dances, masked

A 1951 songbook filled with dozens of songs extolling Turner life contained these verses.

Hei-Lie-Hei-Lo
In question of libation
I hate procrastination
Good things I love to catch
with promptness & dispatch
My throat is dry & rusty
My stomach feels quite musty;
The waiter has, I see,
The medicine for me.

The young ladies are wearing bloomers for their "bar drill" in the gym of the South St. Louis Turnverein. (Photo courtesy of the Missouri Historical Society)

balls, and summer picnics. A stein of beer usually accompanied the social activities and political discussions.

Established after the Civil War, the South St. Louis Turnverein was the second turnverein founded in St. Louis. Eventually German St. Louisans operated eleven turnvereins. The South St. Louis Turnverein, in what was a crowded immigrant neighborhood at the turn of the century, boasted the largest enrollment of young people of any turnverein in the country.

The Turnverein Condominiums building is St. Louis's only remaining nineteenth-century turnverein building.

THIS USED TO BE: A German Gymnastic Club

NOW IT'S: Turnverein Condominiums

LOCATION: 1523 South Tenth Street

St. John's Lofts

Two condominium-filled buildings facing each other on 11th Street near Soulard Market were built during the mid-nineteenth century by a booming and influential Bohemian immigrant community.

Named St. John's Lofts, the condominiums feature Roman arches and tall windows that flood the units with natural light. The buildings housing the loft condos were constructed as the school buildings of St. John Nepomuk Parish, the first Bohemian (or Czech) Roman Catholic parish established outside of Bohemia.

The parish grew into the focal point of a thriving Bohemian neighborhood known as "Bohemian Hill." That neighborhood had begun with a handful of immigrants who fled eastern Europe after the Revolution of 1848 failed. Six years later, they established St. John Nepomuk Catholic Parish in a small frame combination church and school at 11th and Lafayette. As their numbers grew, they built the three-story brick school building at 1621 South 11th Street in 1869 and the additional three-story dark brick school building at 1626 11th Street in 1884. Along with American history and citizenship, the Bohemian language, songs, and traditions were taught in these parish school buildings.

Eventually Bohemian Hill overlapped the Soulard and LaSalle Park neighborhoods. It boasted a Bohemian bakery and butcher shops, Bohemian theater productions, a Bohemian gym (a Sokol), Czech language choirs, and a Czech-language library.

Following World War II, construction of the Darst-Webbe housing project (razed), Interstate 55, and the exchange with Interstate 44 collectively destroyed fifty blocks of the Bohemian Hill neighborhood. Despite the destruction of their neighborhood, Bohemian St. Louisans continue to maintain their historic church, church hall, and rectory. They saved the school buildings by converting them into condominiums.

At the beginning of the twentieth century, the Czech language publishing house on 11th Street (razed) spurred the movement for Bohemian independence leading to the creation of Czechoslovakia.

The St. John's Lofts building, constructed as a Bohemian schcol in 1884. (Photo by Dylan Weber Callahan)

The engraving in the Czech language over the door of the lofts announces that it was the entrance to the schcol and parish hall built in 1884. (Photo by Dylan Weber Callahan)

THIS USED TO BE: Bohemian School Buildings

NOW IT'S: St. John's Lofts

LOCATION: 1621 South 11th Street and 1626 South 11th Street

Obata, a Creative Communications Firm

Within the exposed brick walls of the 120-year-old building at 1614 Menard Street, free-standing office and studio spaces seem to float under the gabled roof. The old mission building that houses Obata, where creative teams develop communications and marketing programs for Fortune 500 companies, was built as a result of the deadly tornado of 1896. The tornado wiped away the hall where a Presbyterian mission had been conducting the largest primary Sunday school class in the world.

That Presbyterian mission had officially organized in 1875 and used the second-floor hall over the old Soulard Market building for classrooms. Enrollment in the mission's Sunday school was reported as 1,537. On May 27, 1896, the tornado tore its way along Lafayette Avenue destroying everything in its path, including the market building. With its classrooms in ruins, the Soulard Market mission Sunday school was "compelled to meet in the waiting room of a Police Station, where tramps slept in winter."[19]

Presbyterians in Pittsburgh helped raise money to construct this Presbyterian mission building that is now home to Obata. (Photo from a private collection)

In 1897, the Presbyterian mission dedicated its new home, the dignified building on Menard Street designed

Following the tornado of 1896, the chief of police stated the significance of the Presbyterian mission: "The restraining influence of the Soulard Market Mission is worth one hundred police men a year to that part of the city."

Members of Markham Memorial Presbyterian Church in a Sunday school classroom ca. 1910. (Photo from a private collection)

by local architects Weber and Grable. In 1901, the mission officially organized as a church. It was named Markham Memorial Presbyterian in honor of the founder of the Sunday school, William Markham. The church served generations of immigrants from eastern Europe and their children.

The construction of Interstate 55 destroyed a swath of housing in the church's neighborhood, forcing out six thousand residents and scattering the membership of Markham Memorial Presbyterian Church. The historic church building was closed in June 1957.

When Obata acquired the old mission in 1980, the building had badly deteriorated. The firm, which had been founded by Kimio Obata (brother of architect Gyo Obata) in 1948, restored the exterior of the old mission while transforming the sanctuary into creative work spaces.

THIS USED TO BE: A Presbyterian Mission

NOW IT'S: Obata, a Creative Communications Firm

LOCATION: 1614 Menard Street

Dutchtown Neighborhood (page 172)

Ely Walker Lofts (page 30)

St. Louis Hills Estates (page 198)

ARCHANGEL

Bailey's Range and Apartments (page 22)

2020 Washington Condominiums (page 26)

Tower Grove Park (page 192)

Saint Louis University's Office of Admissions (page 42)

Westminster Place (page 78)

2 Hortense Place (page 84)

HORTENSE
PLACE
PRIVATE
STREET NOT
THROUGH

City House in Grand Center Arts District (page 40)

Saint Louis University Museum of Art (page 44)

Maryland Plaza (page 82)

Schlafly Tap Room (page 32)

A Mount Pleasant Neighborhood (page 174)

Soulard Preservation Hall

Tall windows topped with stone lintels punctuate the dark brick facade of the Soulard Preservation Hall, a popular venue for events from wedding receptions to conferences. The hall's interior, with its polished oak floors and a lavish cherry wood bar, once housed literature and art classes filled with working-class immigrants. It was built by an educational organization, the Self-Culture Hall Association, in 1895.

The Ethical Society of St. Louis had started the Self-Culture Hall Association about 1888 to furnish the "artisan class" with opportunities for self-improvement. The association first offered programming in the crowded, immigrant-packed northern edge of downtown. With the building of the hall on South 9th Street, the association could serve a second crowded immigrant neighborhood. At the turn of the century, hundreds attended classes each week at the Self-Culture Hall on elocution, debate, mandolin playing, singing, American history, and art. The hall had a collection of about twelve hundred lantern slides to illustrate the lectures.

The classes at the Soulard hall in 1900 were attended by tea and coffee packers, vest makers, hatmakers, salesmen, engineers, a plasterer, clerks, furnace men in mills, bookbinders, and workers in shoe, bag, and tobacco factories.

By the 1920s, the building served the growing community of German Hungarians who had begun settling in Soulard at the turn of the twentieth century. The 1927 St. Louis city directory lists fifteen organizations under the heading "Hungarian Societies 1921 S. 9th."

The societies meeting at the hall in the 1920s included the Hungarian Literary Club and the Hungarian Republican Party of St. Louis.

TOM FAREK
Treas.

BOCKALA
Pres.

MARIANO
Committee

THE MICK-A-DELS

ANNOUNCE

THEIR FIRST INFORMAL

DANCE

At The Newly Decorated

HUNGARIAN HALL

1921 South Ninth Street

Wednesday Night, October 28th, 1925

WITH A PRIZE

CHARLESTON

AND A PRIZE

FOX TROT

featuring

SALLY'S SERENADERS

which have finished a successful season at

WEIZER'S HALL

Don't Fail To Be There!

A Good Time For All!

LADIES 35c

IN ADVANCE

GENTS 50c

MIKE CHABARATZ
Errand Boy

"BABA"
Advertiser

TONY CATANZARA
Circulation

The Soulard neighborhood's Self-Culture Hall has been restored as an events venue. (Photo by NiNi Harris)

The program for a dance at the newly decorated Hungarian Hall on October 28, 1925. (Courtesy of the Missouri Historical Society)

THIS USED TO BE: The Self-Culture Hall

NOW IT'S: Soulard Preservation Hall

LOCATION: 1921 South 9th Street

Barlog-Kuszaj-Zero American Legion Post

Since 1958, the sign on the American Legion Post at South 11th and Sidney Streets has memorialized three young men killed in World War II. They were sons of the Polish community that once thrived in the southeastern corner of the Soulard neighborhood.

Thirty-year-old Sgt. Stanley Kuszaj was killed on the Allied line on December 20, 1944. John Barlog was cut in two by German machine gun fire on the day he arrived at the front lines in the Battle of the Bulge. And twenty-two-year-old Corporal Frank Zero was killed on blood-soaked Okinawa on April 3, 1945.

The austere-looking building that bears the names of Kuszaj, Barlog, and Zero used to be a Second Empire–style town house. William Koenig, who managed his agricultural implements business, built the once elegant town house in 1889.

Six years later, George F. Durant, general manager of the American District Telegraph Company, bought the building. As the licensee of the Bell Telephone Company, he radically altered the home. On building permits, Durant called the building a "telephone station."

Southwestern Bell Telephone Company sold the altered home to a veterans' association in 1941, and in 1958 the American Legion's Barlog-Kuszaj-Zero Post 422 acquired the home.

The center of life of the small Polish community in Soulard was Our Lady of Czestochowa Parish, founded in 1907 at 4th and Victor Streets. It served the Polish immigrants settling near the industries east of Broadway. In 1957, the parish was closed to make room for industrial development.

This Victorian home was converted into a telephone station and later into an American Legion post. (Photo by Emma Prince)

Portrait of German American businessman William Koenig, who built the Second Empire–style house on 11th and Sidney Streets that has been converted into an American Legion post. (Photo from a private collection)

THIS USED TO BE: A Townhome and a "Telephone Station"

NOW IT'S: Barlog-Kuszaj-Zero American Legion Post

LOCATION: 2601 South 11th Street

62 Big Daddy's Bar and Grill

The site of the 120-year-old building that dominates the corner of 10th and Sidney Streets had historic significance long before the St. Louis Brewing Association constructed the three-story brewery and saloon, now Big Daddy's Bar and Grill. When the Civil War was tearing the nation apart in the spring of 1861, Home Guard volunteers stashed up to twelve hundred muskets at that corner to defend the United States of America.

The site of that building and the surrounding property with ball fields and small nineteenth-century buildings was part of Anton Jaeger's beer garden. Beer gardens were popular gathering places for German immigrants, many of whom came to America seeking political freedom. This particular beer garden had a strategic value since it was on high ground near the United States Arsenal. The muskets, cartridges, cannon, and powder stored at the arsenal at Broadway and Arsenal Street could equip an army. Protecting that arsenal was a priority for the Union.

Throughout the secession winter of 1861, supporters of the United States and of abolition were forming Union clubs throughout the city of St. Louis. These clubs organized regiments as the Home Guard. The First Home Guard Regiment, with twelve hundred men in twelve companies, chose Jaeger's Garden for its headquarters and armory.

On May 10, 1861, half the companies of the First Home Guard took up positions guarding the streets and roads leading to the arsenal. The rest of the regiment joined other secret regiments from across the city. Then they moved on the camp of the secessionist state militia, Camp Jackson, in Lindell Grove. They overwhelmed the militia, who surrendered.

The efforts of these German immigrants secured St. Louis for the Union.

The St. Louis Brewing Association constructed the Big Daddy's building as a brewery and saloon in 1897. (Photo by Emma Prince)

Captain Roderick E. Rombauer, one of four Hungarian-immigrant brothers who were loyal to the Union, was a member of the regiment drilling at Anton Yaeger's Beer Garden.

THIS USED TO BE: A Civil War Armory

NOW IT'S: Big Daddy's Bar and Grill

LOCATION: 10th and Sidney Streets

Benton Park

A Victorian pleasure ground, Benton Park's fourteen acres feature an undulating landscape with giant shade trees, wandering walkways, and quaint stone and iron bridges. Opened as a city park at the end of the Civil War, it developed as German Americans were lining the surrounding South City streets with brick town houses, storefronts, and flats. The park-keeper was a German immigrant and horticulturist named Edward Krausnick. Before Krausnick turned the acreage into a mecca for Sunday picnickers and a setting for Saturday night band concerts, grave markers dotted this landscape.

Since 1833, the land had been the City Cemetery. The road it bordered, Arsenal Street, was the early road that led to the federal arsenal on the river. When the cemetery opened, St. Louis's population numbered only 6,397 residents. Most St. Louisans lived on what is now the grounds of the Gateway Arch. The land around the cemetery was only sparsely settled.

Over the next quarter century, the population of St. Louis grew exponentially. Waves of American migrants, Irish immigrants, and German immigrants built neighborhoods reaching north and south from the original village of St. Louis.

By 1856, the city's population rose to more than 125,000. As the city was growing toward the cemetery, the cemetery had been filling with burials of the victims of horrendous cholera epidemics. The burials of cholera victims may have seemed a health threat to the neighborhoods growing nearer. The graves were removed and reburied

Perhaps Krausnick's landscape at Benton Park was inspired by the work of his father, also named Edward Krausnick, who had been landscape gardener at Sans Souci, the summer palace of Frederick the Great in Potsdam, Germany.

Krausnick's lush landscapes in Benton Park are depicted in this postcard. (Postcard from a private collection)

in the quarantine section of Arsenal Island, then located in the Mississippi River near the foot of Arsenal Street.

In 1866, civic leaders dedicated the site of the old City Cemetery as a city park.

THIS USED TO BE: City Cemetery

NOW IT'S: Benton Park

LOCATION: South St. Louis

Senate Square

The blocks of Senate and Congress Streets totally disrupt the grid pattern of the surrounding streets in the Benton Park neighborhood and form a distinctive pocket called Senate Square—once the site of an earthen fort designed to protect St. Louis from Confederate armies.

Unlike the nearby blocks, Senate Square's housing is uniform—built with the same height and setbacks, constructed during the 1880s and 1890s, and featuring elaborate brickwork. The pocket's irregular street pattern and uniform architecture results from its development beginning later than the adjacent blocks. It was delayed until the earthen Civil War fort on the site could be leveled.

President Lincoln appointed Major General John C. Fremont, known as the "Pathfinder" for his trailblazing in the American West, as commander of the western military department headquartered in St. Louis. (Photo courtesy of Missouri Historical Society)

This fort was built at the beginning of the war, when both the Union and the new Confederacy coveted St. Louis. In the spring of 1861, St. Louis's busy port and strategic location on the vast river system made its control critical to both sides of the growing conflict. Even after local Union volunteers, mostly Germans, had overwhelmed and accepted the surrender of the secessionist state militia on May 10, 1861, rebels continued to threaten St. Louis.

To protect the city, Union general John C. Fremont ordered the building of ten earthen forts around its periphery. The forts would serve as rallying points for Union volunteers to defend St. Louis.

Senate Square was the site of Fort No. 3. It had heavy guns and a small attached powder magazine.

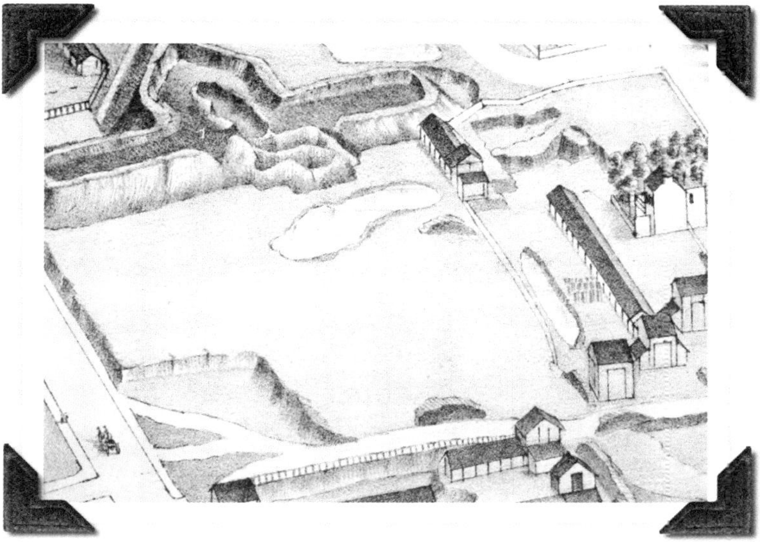

Earthen Fort No. 3 as it appeared in *Pictorial St. Louis*, 1875. The site of the fort became Senate Square, framed by Sidney Street, Lynch Street, and Lemp Avenue and the alley east of McNair Street. (Illustration courtesy of Carondelet Historical Sociaty)

Though never the scene of fighting, these forts may have intimidated secessionists.

THIS USED TO BE: A Civil War Fort

NOW IT'S: Senate Square

LOCATION: South St. Louis

65

The Historic Benton Park Neighborhood

Germanic craftsmen built most of the Benton Park neighborhood and gave it its architectural flair during the late nineteenth century. The neighborhood of small dwellings, grand homes, pocket parks, churches, and breweries boasts more than sixteen hundred historic buildings. Framed by Gravois, Jefferson, Interstate 55, and Cherokee, the entire neighborhood seems shaded a rich red by the color of the nineteenth-century bricks. This charming neighborhood, which now offers eateries and coffeehouses among renovated homes, was not always inviting. It once posed constant threats to police officers.

During the early and mid-twentieth century, migrants from rural areas began settling in the neighborhood. They had fewer urban skills and less education than the earlier generations of neighborhood residents. "Hoosiers" was the derogatory name attached to them.

By the 1960s, the police used caution when approaching many taverns on the near south side, including those in the Benton Park neighborhood. When Charles Marvin came out of the St. Louis Police Academy in 1970, the Benton Park neighborhood had "a tavern on every corner and a fight in every tavern." Marvin remembers, "It was a blue collar neighborhood. People would go in the tavern, and overindulge on Busch's products. Old arguments would arise and booze lubricates the animosity. We [the police] would have to get in there and break up the fights. That's why it was a night stick district."

Marvin would see the same people on their stoops, on the streets, and in the taverns. He remembered, "One night you'd put somebody in jail, and the next night you'd see him walking down the street. The same guy would wave and apologize."

Icarians, French immigrants who had come to America to establish a communal colony, were among the earliest settlers in Benton Park.

Chief Eugene Camp presenting an award to Charles Marvin, with his wife, Judith, at his side, in recognition of Marvin stopping a burglary in progress in the Third District on Easter Sunday, 1971. (Courtesy of Judith Marvin)

Charles Marvin's identification photo taken on his graduation from the St. Louis Police Academy. When he entered the force, the Third District that included the Benton Park neighborhood was considered the city's toughest district. Many Third District residents resolved disputes with their fists. (Courtesy of Judith Marvin)

In recent decades, one building at a time, residents have been restoring the neighborhood's vitality and distinctive nineteenth-century charm.

THIS USED TO BE: A Nightstick Neighborhood

NOW IT'S: The Historic Benton Park Neighborhood

LOCATION: South St. Louis

Victorian Storefront at 1976–82 Arsenal

A mansard roof with ornate dormer windows tops the three-story building facing Arsenal Street next to the Victorian landscape of Benton Park. The storefront and its setting recalls late nineteenth-century St. Louis, when this substantial store building was in an up-and-coming Germanic neighborhood on the city's south side. During its 130-year history, however, the commercial building was not always well maintained. And beginning on April 4, 1968, there were whispers, rumors, and suspicions about its barkeeper/owner and his relationship to his nefarious brother.

By the 1960s, the neighborhood was showing signs of neglect, and the handsome storefront housed the rundown Grape Vine Tavern. Chain-smoking John Ray operated the tavern, which was darkened by its black painted walls. Ray had a bit of a speech impediment, which could make him hard to understand. Most days he'd walk to a nearby convenience store and buy lunch meat and bread for his midday meal. Known only as Jack to his customers, he wiled away hours playing pool with them. Reportedly, Ray's sister leased the tavern. In December 1968, John Ray acquired ownership of the tavern building.

Ray, who seemed older than his thirty-four years, stayed under the radar. He tried to keep his relationship to his brother, assassin James Earl Ray, a secret from the customers in his dismal tavern.

His brother, who was described as a drifter and a typical hoodlum, had escaped from the Missouri State Penitentiary on a bread truck on April 23, 1967. On April 4, 1968, in Memphis, the two-bit felon murdered civil rights leader Dr. Martin Luther King Jr. He had slain the man whose courageous voice had brought about massive social change in the United States.

The storefront that housed Ray's Grape Vine Tavern was built in 1889. (Photo by Emma Prince)

THIS USED TO BE: Grape Vine Tavern

NOW IT'S: A Restored Victorian Storefront at 1976-82 Arsenal

LOCATION: South St. Louis

67

STL Style House

"I'd tell my Marine buddies, if you ever get to St. Louis, I'll have a bar there. So I bought this place a block and a half from my house for $2,750," said Norbert Thurmer, explaining how he opened his corner bar in 1954.[20] The tavern that this marine opened at the corner of Cherokee and Compton reflected the distinctive character of its immediate neighborhood while also becoming St. Louis's first sports bar.

In 1958, Thurmer sponsored ten bowling teams. He also sponsored soccer, basketball, and rugby teams. His nickname, "Mr. Softie," came from his love of men's fast-pitch softball. Thurmer's softball teams were powerhouses from the 1950s to the 1980s.

Old soccer players, neighborhood residents, lawyers, police officers, and brewery executives filled the barstools and crowded the tables at Thurmer's. Saint Louis University basketball players supposedly had jobs in the kitchen, but Thurmer described what the players did as "mostly eating."[21]

Along with the eclectic crowd, steak sandwiches, and beer that seemed to flow as fast as at Busch Stadium, Thurmer's was known for its humor-filled atmosphere. Everything about it became legendary, like the customers responding to the Rose Bowl having a Rose Bowl queen with Thurmer's having a Toilet Bowl queen.

After thirty-four years as a neighborhood institution, tax problems forced the closing of Thurmer's in 1989. (Sports broadcaster Bob Costas emceed a fund-raiser to help with Thurmer's IRS problems.)

In 2010, STL Style House, with collectibles and souvenirs for people who love St. Louis, opened in the historic corner storefront.

A German American couple—Joseph and Clara Venverloh, who owned and operated a Cherokee Street shoe store—constructed the historic storefront in 1913. During the early twentieth century, the storefront housed a dry goods store, a restaurant, and a liquor store.

Thurmer's Tavern is now home to STL Style House, offering custom-made items that celebrate St. Louis. Proprietors Randy and Jeff Vines see St. Louis as a work of art. They proudly state, "This town is overflowing with idiosyncrasies, and that unique local flavor should be a source of pride." (Photo by Emma Prince)

THIS USED TO BE: Thurmer's Tavern, St. Louis's First Sports Bar

NOW IT'S: STL Style House

LOCATION: 3159 Cherokee Street

Hammond's Books

The nooks and crannies of the Victorian-era storefront at 1939 Cherokee Street are filled with shelves of rare, collectible, and specialty books. A destination for booklovers for more than thirty-five years, Hammond's Books also enchants casual visitors who stumble into this treasure trove of more than two hundred thousand books. However, it appears that this charming shop building once secretly housed an illegal business.

German Americans Rosina and Jacob Keller bought the lot on Cherokee in 1888 and built the store with their home upstairs. After Jacob died in 1893, Rosina married another German immigrant, Protas Mayer, who worked as a brewer. While Protas and Rosina lived in the second-floor apartment, Rosina turned the first-floor storefront into a boardinghouse. With the Lemp Brewery only a block away and the Anheuser-Busch brewery close by, 1939 Cherokee was an ideal location to operate a boardinghouse for brewery workers. The 1910 census lists eight boarders, all German immigrants, living on the first floor. Seven of the eight worked at a brewery.

Prohibition eliminated Protas's job and emptied out Rosina's boardinghouse business. Protas, a skilled brewer, found work as a day laborer.

There is no evidence that the Mayers found legitimate employment or established a legal business to replace their lost income. Skills, attitudes, and physical evidence, however, suggest that the Mayers did develop a way to restore the family income (though perhaps not through legal means).

Protas knew how to make beer. Many law-abiding German immigrants, as well as naturalized citizens from all over Europe, believed Prohibition was absurd. They ignored it, producing wine, beer, whiskey, gin, and vodka in their basements for both personal use and for sale.

When Jovanka and Peter Hammond bought the storefront in 1981 to open their bookstore, they found a suspicious door in the basement. The door opened into a narrow, short tunnel lined with irregular concrete walls that led to a small room under the backyard.

The building housing Hammond's Antiques & Books at 1939 Cherokee Street was built in 1889. (Photo by Emma Prince)

A hatch opened through the low ceiling into the yard. One piece of equipment was in the room—a bottle capper.

THIS USED TO BE: A Bootlegger's Brewery?

NOW IT'S: Hammond's Books

LOCATION: 1939 Cherokee Street

69

The Mud House

The popular coffee shop and eatery known as the Mud House operates out of a Victorian-era corner storefront and its stone-walled courtyard. The storefront was built as a German neighborhood grocery store—the American dream of one immigrant family.

Early in 1891, German immigrant Adam Seyler purchased the corner lot on Cherokee Street and Illinois Avenue. Seyler, who had immigrated to the United States at age fourteen, had only been in this country for a decade when he bought the corner property and constructed the substantial building. It had space for two stores on the first floor and apartments on the second and third floors. Coal-fueled, cast-iron stoves heated the apartments and stores, and gas fixtures provided the lighting.

Seyler operated a grocery store in the first-floor commercial space, and he and his German immigrant wife, Rosa, raised their growing family in their home on the second floor. Eventually they had three daughters and three sons. By 1900, not only were Adam and Rosa proprietors of their own business, but they had paid off the mortgage on their combined home and commercial space.

After Adam passed away in 1909, Rosa managed the store, though she had to mortgage their storefront and home.

World War I altered the American experience for many immigrant families, especially Germans like the Seylers. All three of Adam and Rosa's sons joined the United States military in the fight to defeat their ancestral homeland, Germany. Two of their sons were left partially disabled.

Philip Seyler, an infantryman, served overseas from September 1918 to August 1919. Albert Seyler was inducted in July 1918 and left with a 40 percent disability. Jacob Seyler was severely wounded in action, leaving him with a 60 percent disability.

The storefront's wide doorways allowed for hauling bushels of potatoes and bulk sacks of flour from the backs of wagons into the building when it was a German American grocery store. (Photo by Emma Prince)

THIS USED TO BE: A Grocery Store—A German's "American Dream"

NOW IT'S: The Mud House

LOCATION: 2101 Cherokee Street

Cornerstone Center for Early Education

The sounds of 150 young children playing and learning emanate from the Cornerstone Center for Early Education, housed in the storefront at 39th Street and Russell Boulevard. Eight decades ago, when the storefront housed a neighborhood grocery store, the sounds of streetcars and church bells were the musical backdrop at that corner.

During the 1930s and 1940s, the Hackman family lived in a flat over their family business—Hackman Grocery, at 3901 Russell Boulevard. Carolyn Hackman, who grew up over the store, described her family's business.

"Most things came in bulk then—rice, beans, dried peas. . . . I can remember Uncle Lou working at the counter weighing pound and large amounts into brown bags which were originally tied with string. . . . Another counter was full of bins for coffee, tea, and spices." Orders were filled on the "long marble-topped counter with a black metal dispenser for a huge roll of brown paper at the end."

"Farmer Meyer came in regularly with fresh things from his farm [at about Highway 40 and Mason Road today] and Tony Lombardo came . . . with produce from Produce Row." The "bananas came by the entire stalk which would hang near the front door with a curved knife handy to cut off the exact number required."

When Hackman was growing up, "the hourly chimes from St. Margaret's were part of the neighborhood sounds, like the street cars. . . . "

When 39th Street was a streetcar route, the businesses in small storefronts along the street could answer all the daily needs of Shaw neighborhood residents. In 1935, the 39th Street storefronts housed grocers, bakers, confectionaries, butcher shops, restaurants, shoe repair shops, a cleaners, a laundry, and a poultry store.

For decades, this handsome Shaw neighborhood storefront housed the family run Hackman Grocery. (Photo by NiNi Harris)

"The Park Avenue street car ran along 39th Street. . . . The sound of the cars was so normal we weren't even aware of it until we had such a severe snow storm that they didn't run. I remember waking up and wandering why everything was so quiet."[22]

THIS USED TO BE: Hackman Grocery in the Shaw Neighborhood

NOW IT'S: Cornerstone Center for Early Education

LOCATION: 3901 Russell Boulevard

Morgan Ford Business District

The Amsterdam bar, catering to raucous international soccer fans, and the elegant London Tea Room are among the businesses in century-old storefronts lining the energetic Morgan Ford business district. This quarter mile of urban landscape stretches from Morgan Ford's origin at Tower Grove Park south to where the road crosses over the old MoPac railroad tracks at Fyler Avenue. The Missouri Botanical Garden cleared the 6.38 acres adjacent to the tracks at Morgan Ford to develop its new Hardy Plant Nursery.

A century ago, industrial shops covered the plant nursery's site. The then new frame and brick storefronts on Morgan Ford housed neighborhood services like bakeries, hardware stores, doctors' offices, and saloons.

In the 1870s, however, that stretch of Morgan Ford was the dirt road leading to the Parker, Russell Manufacturing Company, with its coal mining operations, then clay mining and fire clay works, and the Oak Hill Fruit Company. A young, rambunctious Charles Marion Russell—the scion of the family that founded and developed the Parker, Russell Manufacturing Company—used to ride his pony down Morgan Ford, whooping and stirring up dust.

Born in 1864, his fondness for playing hooky did not bode well for young Charles Marion Russell's prospects. He was sent off to military school in New Jersey. His dreams, however, were filled with the stories of his grand uncles, who were important figures in the opening of the American West. In 1880, he headed for Montana. He would become one of the greatest artists of the American West and earn the nickname, "the Cowboy Artist."

Charles Marion Russell's grand uncle, William Bent, built and managed Bent's Fort, a trading post on the Santa Fe Trail that was a second home to mountain men and scouts from 1833 until the Mexican War.

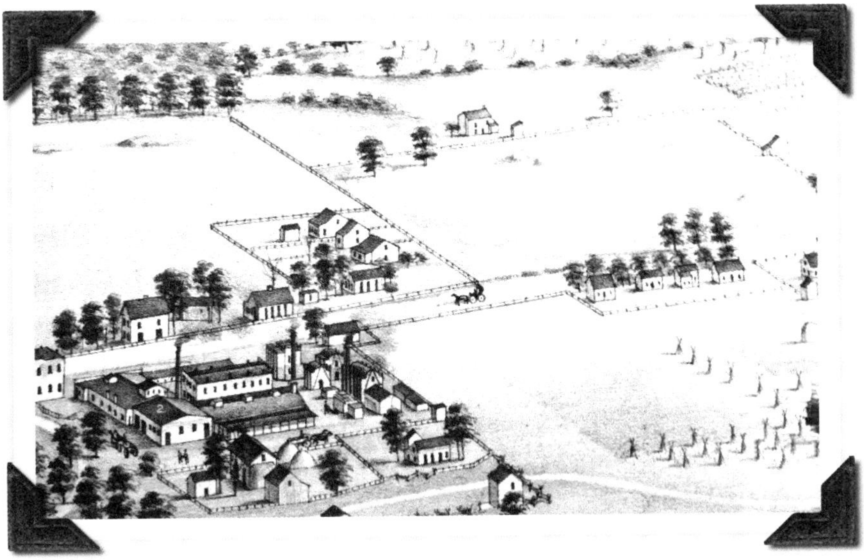

This plate from *Pictorial St. Louis* shows Morgan Ford, then Russell Avenue, leading to the Parker, Russell & Co. in 1875 (Illustration courtesy of Carondelet Historical Society)

THIS USED TO BE: The Playground of the "the Cowboy Artist"

NOW IT'S: Morgan Ford Business District

LOCATION: South St. Louis

Moth Repellent and Urinal Cake Manufactory

Tall brick smokestacks rise out of the cityscape north of Interstate 44 at Grand Avenue. These towers rise from a series of monumental warehouses that had been built for St. Louis's once huge tobacco industry, along Park Avenue just west of Cardinal Glennon Children's Hospital.

Willert Home Products uses most of the five-story brick warehouses as their factories, where the company manufactures urinal cakes, air fresheners, and moth repellents. In these buildings, Willert produces Ty-D-Bol toilet bowl cleaners and exports the bowl fresheners to Japan. The St. Louis–based company employs almost two hundred workers on Park Avenue.

The enormous warehouses, however, were built long before Willert was founded as a family business in 1946. Permits to construct the warehouses were issued to then St. Louis–based Liggett & Myers Tobacco Company in 1895–96. The size of the Liggett & Myers Tobacco Manufacturing Company on Park Avenue indicates the enormous scale of the tobacco industry in St. Louis at the turn of the century and the preeminence of Liggett & Myers in that local industry. John Edmund Liggett was born in St. Louis in 1826 and guided the company for decades, incorporating it as the Liggett & Myers Tobacco Manufacturing Company in 1878.

By 1899, only three years after construction of the plant on Park Avenue, the tobacco factories of St. Louis employed more than four thousand people, many of them women and girls. The average earnings of these workers were $328 a year. During the early decades of the twentieth century, Italians from the growing neighborhood known as "the Hill" found work in these giant warehouses. Polish immigrants from

Tobacco was manufactured in frontier St. Louis by 1817. By 1888, the city was hailed as the largest tobacco manufacturing city in the world.

Exquisitely crafted tobacco warehouses on Park Avenue. (Photo by Dylan Weber Callahan)

Stars made of terra-cotta, an emblem of Star Tobacco, decorate the walls of the old Liggett & Myers tobacco warehouses. (Photo by Dylan Weber Callahan)

Old North St. Louis and from Kosciusko (the southeastern corner of the Soulard neighborhood) daily walked to the plants on Park Avenue where they worked as stemmers, stripping the stems from moistened tobacco leaves.

THIS USED TO BE: Liggett & Myers Tobacco Company

NOW IT'S: Moth Repellent and Urinal Cake Manufactory

LOCATION: 4044 Park Avenue

An Apartment Complex

Apartments fill the imposing three-story red-brick building at Grand Boulevard and Shenandoah Avenue. The sculptural portraits of Mozart, Wagner, and Beethoven that decorate the building's upper walls date to its original use as a music conservatory.

At the beginning of the twentieth century, the clear notes of piano études, the drumbeat of military bands, and melodies formed by well-trained voices floated from the windows of this building when it housed the Strassberger Conservatory of Music.

In 1904, Clement Strassberger chose Otto Wilhelmi, a prominent South City German American architect, to design his new conservatory building on South Grand Boulevard. Strassberger, a German immigrant himself, had begun his music conservatories in the heart of the German community of North St. Louis in 1886. At the turn of the century, he expanded his music classes to serve the south side German community.

Classical music, music history, deportment, physical culture, dramatic art, languages, and ballroom dancing were studied in Strassberger's studios and halls. Enrollment in Strassberger's conservatories reached 1,148 students during the height of the St. Louis German community's political and artistic energy.

As the American public rallied to fight against Germany and the Central Powers in World War I, Strassberger's students and faculty joined the American armed services. Anti-German sentiment, new musical styles, and later competition from radio and talking movies all took their toll on the German conservatory. Enrollment dwindled and eventually the conservatory closed. Through the mid-twentieth century, the building was underused. It barely stirred a memory of the vibrant cultural life that had once surrounded it.

During World War I, a wave of anti-German sentiment intimidated German Americans. St. Louisans stopped speaking the German language on the street.

This postcard of the Strassberger Conservatory dates to the beginning of the twentieth century when Grand Boulevard was the cultural spine of South City. (Postcard from a private collection)

Community leaders, however, recognized the beauty and significance of the elegant conservatory and restored it as the Strassberger Court Apartments in 1984.

THIS USED TO BE: Strassberger Conservatory of Music

NOW IT'S: An Apartment Complex

LOCATION: 2306 South Grand

Beck Avenue in South St. Louis

A hodgepodge of frame houses with gabled roofs are set on large, irregular lots along the 4300 and 4400 blocks of Beck Avenue in South St. Louis. Some of the houses are set at the back of the lots, and some are at angles to the street. Newer brick houses are scattered among the earlier generations of housing. This street doesn't feel like the rest of South St. Louis because its origins are as a nineteenth-century mining town settled by immigrants from Great Britain.

In the 1820s, miners from England, Scotland, Ireland, and Wales began immigrating to work in the Russell family's coal mining operations based around Morgan Ford Road and Tholozan Avenue. Some were British miners who were already working in other parts of the United States when they heard that there were opportunities at the coal mines in South St. Louis. A few of the miners had been heading to California for the gold rush when they ran out of money. They found work at the Russell coal mines.

They bought parcels along Beck Avenue and built humble frame homes. They nurtured orchards and grew vegetables on their big lots. Some raised chickens. Everyone in the settlement enjoyed the flower garden raised by Mrs. Hazeldine, the settlement's midwife, in her four-acre yard. Many of the homes were actually along "the Alley," which was the alley or dirt path between Beck and Chippewa. (A few houses still stand on the alley.)

The settlement became known as Beckville and the road Beck Avenue for German immigrant Frederick Beck, who operated a store with a post office on Morgan Ford at the edge of the settlement.

The advertisement for Frederick Beck's store in Pitzman's 1878 atlas reads, "Dealer in Dry Goods, Groceries, Provisions and General Notions, Saloon, etc."

An engraving from a drawing of the "picturesque" coal mining operations near Gravois Road, ca. 1855. The cost of coal at the pits was ten cents per bushel.(Illustration courtesy of Missouri Historical Society)

Descendants of early settlers stayed in Beckville for a century. As the city gradually surrounded them, their large yards were subdivided, and new housing built where there had been gardens.

THIS USED TO BE: Beckville, a Mining Town

NOW IT'S: Beck Avenue in South St. Louis

LOCATION: South St. Louis

75

U-Haul

Rising seven stories above a viaduct over Gravois at Meramec Street, the giant tan brick U-Haul facility dominates its South St. Louis cityscape. The building's huge windows expose the interior's long corridors lined with orange doors for individual storage units. While the orange doors are characteristic of U-Haul facilities, the terra-cotta panel over the old doorway reveals the storage building's original use as a candy factory.

The octagonal, terra-cotta panel features colorful sculptural reliefs of candies, including red and white candy canes and peppermint-colored Life Savers.

Candy manufacturer Vincent L. Price, father of movie star Vincent Price, formed a partnership with two other small candy manufacturers in 1902, creating the National Candy Company. They spurred the success of their sweet endeavor with an exhibit at the 1904 World's Fair.

National Candy specialized in manufacturing jawbreakers and jelly beans, true joys of childhood. The company had twenty-two factories around the United States. In 1927, the company constructed the 300,000-square-foot factory facing Gravois to consolidate its nine St. Louis factories in one building. The new Gravois factory was air-conditioned, allowing candy manufacturing throughout the hot summer months.

The St. Louis–based company, which was one of the nation's largest candy manufacturers, was purchased by Chase Candy in 1948.

Vincent Price, the fourth child of jelly bean entrepreneur Vincent L. Price Sr., began his acting career on stage in London. The menacing tone in his voice earned the young actor roles in film noir, mystery, and horror classics. He became known as the "King of Horror."

The terra-cotta panel over the entrance to the National Candy Company. (Photo by Dylan Weber Callahan)

THIS USED TO BE: A Candy Factory

NOW IT'S: U-Haul

LOCATION: 4230 Gravois

A Dutchtown Neighborhood

A wedge-shaped pocket of the Dutchtown neighborhood is filled with storefronts, apartments, homes, and flats built following World War I. The rough-textured, dark brick used on many of the buildings contrasts with their white stone steps, lintels, and porches. This eye-catching mix of the limestone and matte brick makes this pocket typical of South St. Louis's architecture of the Roaring Twenties.

Before World War I, however, this pocket framed by South Grand Avenue, Meramec Street, and Gasconade Street was the site of a private park featuring a velodrome. The northwest corner of Grand and Meramec (catty-corner from the Feasting Fox) served as the entrance to Priester's Park.

Priester's Park, originally called Hashagen's Park, was sometimes referred to as an amusement park. It offered picnickers a merry-go-round, dance hall, theater, bar, bowling alley, pool tables, and a motion picture booth. Its unique attraction, however, was a frame velodrome or motordrome with a quarter-mile tract. Its steeply banked walls reached up to wooden bleachers. The structure was twenty-four feet tall and boasted a seating capacity of fifty thousand, more than Sportsman's Park.

While the structure could be used as a velodrome for bicyclists, photos suggest that it was a destination for young people racing motorized bicycles, or early motorcycles.

Members of St. Pius V Parish, founded on South Grand in 1906, held their annual parish picnics at Hashagen's Park, then Priester's Park. Parishioners who did not want to walk to the picnic took the streetcar for a nickel.

This photo of a cyclist in the velodrome at Priester's Park was taken by Dutchtown neighborhood amateur photographer and cycling enthusiast Frank Eike about 1914. (Photo courtesy of the Carondelet Historical Society)

Priester's Park was the site of popular balloon ascensions. (Photo courtesy of the Carondelet Historical Society)

THIS USED TO BE: The Motordrome

NOW IT'S: A Dutchtown Neighborhood

LOCATION: South St. Louis

77

A Mount Pleasant Neighborhood

The square of land in the Mount Pleasant neighborhood framed by Itaska and Mount Pleasant Streets and Compton and Virginia Avenues has a grid of streets edged with limestone curbs, narrow tree lawns, granitoid sidewalks, and terraced front yards. Brick flats and cottages with stone stoops and doorways set behind recessed porches fill the city blocks. Storefronts face Virginia Avenue. Most of the buildings date to the beginning of the twentieth century.

Though it may look like the rest of the area, in 1910 or 1920 or 1930 neighbors passing on these streets would have greeted one another in Polish. They would have enjoyed poppy seed stollens on Sunday mornings and *paczki* (a Polish version of jelly donuts) before Lent brought fasting.

A Polish priest, Father Viktor Stepka, and a Polish St. Louisan, August Marchlewski, planned this Polish village in South City. Marchlewski mortgaged his own home to loan Father Stepka the money to buy the then vacant blocks in 1903. The priest subdivided the blocks, selling the individual lots to Polish Americans who were then living in crowded tenements wedged between factories. The list of individuals who purchased the building lots from Father Stepka reads like a Warsaw phone book—Waslewski, Kolozej, Jurkiewicz, Kalinowski, Skredynski, Smugay, Wisnewski, Kwiatkowski. . . .

After the loan was repaid, the profits from the sale of the individual lots helped pay to build a new Polish Catholic parish in the subdivision, named St. Hedwig. The Poles built a combined church and school at 3214 Pulaski Street.

In 1957, the St. Hedwig congregation built a new church facing the corner, one of St. Louis's best examples of mid-century modern architecture. In 2005, the St. Louis Archdiocese closed the parish and sold the church.

The St. Hedwig Parish production of "Polski Uncle Sam" or "Polish Uncle Sam" represented the merging of American culture and Polish culture in South City's Polish subdivision. (Photo from a private collection)

Young members of the Polish dance troupe of St. Hedwig's Parish in the Mount Pleasant neighborhood costumed to dance the Krakowiak in 1929. (Photo from a private collection)

Among the neighborhood entrepreneurs was a Polish American attorney and a Polish art glass studio, Olszewski Art Glass Co. As more Poles moved into the surrounding streets, Hiawatha Street, which cut through the subdivision, was renamed Pulaski Street.

THIS USED TO BE: A Polish Subdivision

NOW IT'S: A Mount Pleasant Neighborhood

LOCATION: South St. Louis

Virginia Avenue

The mile-long stretch of Virginia Avenue between Meramec Street in Dutchtown and Bates Street at the edge of the Carondelet neighborhood used to be known as Stringtown Road.

The road followed a natural ridge in the terrain that was the border of the old Carondelet Common Fields. It evolved during the early nineteenth century as a shortcut between the German settlement on the high ground at Meramec and the Creole village of Carondelet. The small brick German settler's house at 4416 Virginia is the lone building that dates to the scattered settlement or "stringtown" that developed along the road before the Civil War.

Decades later, a grid of streets was superimposed on the landscape and across Stringtown Road, creating triangular and trapezoidal shaped blocks bordering the old road. Adolphus Busch filled the two prominent triangular blocks with delightful, wedge-shaped buildings—the charming Bavarian-style Stork Inn building at 4527 Virginia and the Virginia Show at 5117 Virginia, with its dome roofed entrance. (The Stork Inn was designed to promote the brewery's Malt Nutrine, a health drink, and the Virginia Show was built to present live theater.) These buildings dominated the streetscape and became instant landmarks.

South City Germans lined the blocks in between the landmarks with flats and storefronts. Some had wedge-shaped lawns, and some buildings were built with trapezoidal footprints to fit the angle of the street. The result of the urban development of the rural shortcut known as Stringtown Road is an endlessly fascinating streetscape.

Klipstein and Rathmann designed both the Stork Inn and the Virginia Show in 1910. The firm also designed the Feasting Fox, Bevo Mill, and the Bauernhof at Grant's Farm for Adolphus Busch.

The Hopkins atlas of St. Louis shows a grid of development superimposed around Stringtown Road in 1883. The result was wedge-shaped or trapezoidal-shaped blocks. (Map courtesy of St. Louis Public Library)

The Bavarian-style Stork Inn has a wedge-shaped footprint, filling the wedged block created by Stringtown Road. (Courtesy of architect Tony Duncan)

This early German settler's house was built before the Civil War, when scattered housing along an early shortcut created a "stringtown." (Photo by NiNi Harris)

THIS USED TO BE: Stringtown Road

NOW IT'S: Virginia Avenue

LOCATION: South St. Louis

79

Polish Clubhouse

The stone clubhouse of the Polish National Alliance (PNA) looks like a mix of a mid-century modern ranch house and a Mexican-inspired hacienda. Adding to its mystery is its location—an isolated corner in an industrial area east of Broadway in far South St. Louis.

When neighborhood residents Clarence and Amelia Placht bought the then vacant corner in 1949, a residential neighborhood dating to the nineteenth-century Irish immigration still thrived around it. With the help of his father, a German American stone mason, Clarence set out to build a neighborhood tavern, "the Stone Bar." When St. Columbkille Church was razed, the father and son team salvaged stone from the foundation walls of the Irish church that dated to 1872. Using their station wagon, they hauled the stones a few at a time to 8201 Vulcan. They used the irregular sized limestones to construct their tavern building, which included a low-pitched gabled roof that made the bar look like a 1950s ranch house. To build the stone railing of the roofed porch that stretched along the facade, the duo used granite and marble tombstones rescued when the old St. Marcus Cemetery on Gravois was being cleared.

The unique building's use as the Stone Bar was short-lived. Clarence and Amelia converted the commercial building constructed of historic salvage into their home. As they raised a loving daughter and lived out their lives in the stone house, surrounding industries expanded, erasing most of the nearby residences.

The roots of the PNA go back to 1880 when it was founded as a fraternal organization to provide insurance protection for Polish Americans. The PNA eventually offered insurance and investment programs and youth and sports programs, and it encouraged the preservation of Polish culture. Polish Americans in St. Louis formed Lodge 1134 in 1908.

The Polish National Alliance clubhouse. (Photo by NiNi Harris)

St. Louis's PNA Cadet Lodge 1134, which is known locally among a generation that learned to play soccer through their programs, bought the building in 2014. Volunteers with the PNA have been restoring its interior to its early 1950s appearance when it was the Stone Bar.

THIS USED TO BE: Pieces of St. Columbkille Church and St. Marcus Cemetery

NOW IT'S: Polish Clubhouse

LOCATION: 8201 Vulcan

Pasta Plant and Barge Line

In the southeast corner of St. Louis, where Davis Street stops at the railroad tracks east of Broadway, a sign reads "private property." Behind that sign and beyond a half dozen sets of tracks, barges and tows are moored on the banks of the Mississippi. Many of the barges are riding high, waiting to be loaded at American Commercial Lines, a century-old company that moves minerals, grains, and petrochemicals by river. The company also transports wind turbines for energy-efficient wind farms.

The giant grain elevators of Italgrani USA line the riverbank just north of the barge operations. With a capacity of four million bushels, Italgrani's elevators and wheat mills supply the wheat for pasta, puddings, and breakfast cereals.

The commercial activity evidences the powerful role that the Mississippi River plays in St. Louis's twenty-first-century economy, as it did during the twentieth and nineteenth centuries. And during the Civil War, that specific site at the end of Davis Street was the scene of tremendous industry focused on winning the war for the Union.

In August 1861, self-taught river engineer James B. Eads, who would design and build the Eads Bridge following the Civil War, leased the boatyards at the foot of Davis Street for his Union Iron Works. Immediately, he employed hundreds of craftsmen and laborers at the iron works, which covered the two blocks lining the river extending north of Davis Street. The air reverberated with the clank of their hammers and the pounding of iron and steel. In only three months, Eads launched the first of his revolutionary ironclads at this site. In addition to building the ironclads, Eads produced another twenty-five gunboats and forty mortar rafts with siege guns at the Davis Street boatyards.

General US Grant used Eads's wooden, steam-powered paddle wheelers covered with protective iron coats in the Battles of Fort Henry, Fort Donelson, and Memphis and the Siege of Vicksburg.

The Union ironclad USS *Saint Louis*, later renamed *DeKalb*, built by James B. Eads in the Carondelet boat yards. (Courtesy of the Carondelet Historical Society)

River engineer James B. Eads. (Photo from a private collection)

General Ulysses S. Grant used the ironclads and rafts built at the Union Iron Works to gain control of the Mississippi, cutting the Confederacy in two.

THIS USED TO BE: Civil War Boatyards

NOW IT'S: Pasta Plant and Barge Line

LOCATION: South St. Louis

81

A Private Residence

A rusticated stone retaining wall wraps around the corner at Michigan Avenue and Kraus Street as it did during the secession winter of 1860–61. On the terrace above that wall sits a large brick home (6727 Michigan), painted to protect its soft, handmade brick from the elements.

In the spring of 1861, a settlement of Germans existed a few blocks south of this house. They were staunch supporters of the Union. Just southeast on the riverbank were the boatyards where engineer James B. Eads would soon be building ironclads for the Union.

The man who called 6727 Michigan home, however, was dedicated to secession.

John Stevens Bowen was a native of Georgia. After graduating from West Point, he was assigned to Jefferson Barracks in St. Louis, where he met and married a local girl, Mary Kennerly. He became an architect in pre–Civil War St. Louis and designed and built his family home at 6727 Michigan.

His family life, his social life, and his successful career as an architect came to an abrupt end with the Confederates firing on Fort Sumter on April 12, 1861. Along with other Missouri secessionists, Bowen left St. Louis to fight for the Confederacy. His skills quickly advanced him to the rank of major general.

By the fall of 1862, the war in the West focused on the city of Vicksburg, a citadel guarding the Mississippi River for the Confederacy. It sat atop the river bluffs with swampy terrain on other sides. General Bowen engineered the defenses linking the swamps and

General Bowen and General Grant were acquaintances before the war. The Union general, who would eventually command an army of a million men, used to deliver firewood in Bowen's neighborhood.

The home of Confederate general John Stevens Bowen. (Photo by NiNi Harris)

bluffs, making Vicksburg almost unconquerable.

The determined general Ulysses S. Grant maneuvered his armies for months until he circled Vicksburg. Then he bombarded the city for forty-seven days, until the Confederates surrendered the city on July 4, 1863. With Union control of the Mississippi, the Confederacy was cut in two.

General Bowen never returned to his home at 6727 Michigan Avenue. After the fall of Vicksburg, he was stricken with dysentery and died on July 13, 1863.

THIS USED TO BE: The Home of a Confederate General

NOW IT'S: A private residence

LOCATION: 6727 Michigan Avenue

Water Fountain in the Ivory Triangle

The streets meet at angles forming wedge-shaped blocks in the Ivory Triangle, the historic German area of South City's Carondelet neighborhood. The focal point is a triangular block framed by Ivory Avenue, Virginia Avenue, and Schirmer Street that serves as a mini commemorative park. It includes a flagpole and a bust of neighborhood leader Albert "Red" Villa. The son of Italian immigrants, Villa served as alderman for the Carondelet neighborhood from 1953 to 1990.

The centerpiece of the civic space is a water fountain with the water spraying into a large round pool. During the late nineteenth century, this iron pool served as a trough to water horses.

The wedge-shaped piece of land belonged to Daniel Paule (1831–1897), who operated a general store and a hay and grain business across the street at 7700 Ivory Avenue. Since hay and grain were bulky purchases, locals made Paule's store their last stop of the day, and by then their horses usually needed watering. Customers left their wagons in the triangle and walked through Paule's store to get buckets of water from his stable out back. Then they carried the overflowing buckets back through the store. Unsavory characters hung around who would water horses for a tip. They were continually trekking through his business.

Paule decided to stop this nuisance by giving the wedge of land to the city as a site for a horse watering trough. The gift had a restriction that "it shall remain, forever, as such. Otherwise its ownership shall revert to his heirs."

During the twentieth century, with no need for a horse watering trough, the city converted it to a fountain.

A much smaller horse trough has survived in Lafayette Park near the statue of George Washington. It has been converted into a raised planter.

The water fountain in Carondelet's Ivory Triangle. (Photo by Emma Prince)

THIS USED TO BE: A Horse Trough

NOW IT'S: Water Fountain in the Ivory Triangle

LOCATION: South St. Louis

83

Carondelet Historical Society

The home of the Carondelet Historical Society is a former St. Louis Public School that served as the cradle of the kindergarten movement in the United States. With the building's facade carefully restored to its Victorian-era appearance and the classrooms converted into museum rooms dedicated to local history, there is no evidence that the school that was converted into a museum was once a neighborhood bar and grill.

When the Des Peres School opened in the fall of 1873, revolutionary educator Susan Blow was conducting an experimental kindergarten in one of the school's four classrooms. As she taught the kindergartners, she also trained young women in the philosophy of the kindergarten movement. These young women helped her open more kindergartens in St. Louis Public Schools and then spread the kindergarten movement across the nation.

In 1935, when kindergartens were an accepted part of American education, the St. Louis Public School system closed the then sixty-two-year-old Des Peres School.

The school building sat vacant for twelve years before a local insurance man bought it and converted the building into a commercial venture housing the Kindergarten Grill, the Bark Bar, and meeting rooms. The grill, open every day except Sunday, served breakfast, lunch, and dinner. The large hall, which could seat 250 people, rented for monthly meetings for as little as $12.50 per meeting.

Twelve years later, a grocery chain bought the old school and built a modern one-story grocery store onto the school's side. To turn the

The Des Peres School served the Carondelet neighborhood, the southernmost neighborhood of the city of St. Louis. Originally an independent French village, Carondelet was annexed by booming St. Louis in 1870.

Martinis cost fifty cents and a Thanksgiving dinner of turkey with mushroom dressing and cranberry sauce cost $1.85 at the Kindergarten Grill. (Courtesy of the Carondelet Historical Society)

Victorian-era school into the grocery store's warehouse, the market operators filled the window openings with concrete blocks and tore up the pine floors to install conveyor belts.

In 1981, the Carondelet Historical Society purchased the building and undertook the tedious and slow mission of restoring the facade of the old Des Peres School to its 1873 appearance—preserving this landmark in American education.

THIS USED TO BE: Kindergarten Grill and Bark Bar

NOW IT'S: Carondelet Historical Society

LOCATION: 6303 Michigan Avenue

84

Boulevard Heights Neighborhood

Hansel and Gretel–style brick cottages and small ranch houses with driveways leading to carports line the streets of the Boulevard Heights neighborhood. Businesses are rare in this quiet neighborhood that wraps around the south and west sides of Carondelet Park in South City.

During the early decades of the twentieth century, before the subdivisions, much of the Boulevard Heights neighborhood south of the park was known as Cow Shit Hill. That name was an accurate depiction of the high ground south of Carondelet Park, where dairy farmers grazed their cows.

The Knackstedt family brought their dairy cows with them in 1889 when they moved into the two-story frame house on the hill, at 3666 Upton Street at the corner of Eugene Avenue. George Knackstedt, who was only four years old at the time of the move, recalled life on the dairy farm: "[A] seven-day week—up at dawn and to bed with the chickens. Milk was delivered 2 times a day in a wagon. No bottles then: a dipper, a milk can and a bell were standard equipment."

George Knackstedt worked on and ran the family dairy for six decades. In 1915, he sold the cows, but he continued to operate the dairy with milk shipped by rail from dairy farmers around De Soto, Hillsboro, and Pevely. During World War II, he was kept busy helping supply Jefferson Barracks, where thousands of young Americans were in training.

In 1954, George Knackstedt's health failed, and he sold the dairy. The Knackstedt Dairy building on Upton at Eugene is one of the few commercial buildings in the Boulevard Heights neighborhood.

In addition to dairy farms, there were truck farms and even a mushroom farm in the neighborhood. In 1911, two of the area farms cleared $10,000 each on their strawberry crops.

A Knackstedt milk wagon making deliveries in the nearby Carondelet neighborhood. (Courtesy of the Carondelet Historical Society)

An ad for Knackstedt Farm Dairy Co. that appeared in the 1929 Cleveland High School *Beacon*. (Courtesy of the Carondelet Historical Society)

THIS USED TO BE: Cow Shit Hill

NOW IT'S: Boulevard Heights Neighborhood

LOCATION: South St. Louis

85

Private Residence on The Hill and the Columbia Foundation for the Visual Arts

The story of the combination home and art gallery on Columbia Avenue on The Hill, originally a movie house, reflects the meteoric rise of a hardworking Greek immigrant family and is tied to twentieth-century motion picture empires.

In 1925, the city of St. Louis issued Greek American George Skouras a permit to construct a $55,000 theater, the Columbia, that could accommodate both stage shows and silent films. At the time of the construction of this neighborhood movie house at 5329–33 Columbia on The Hill, the Skouras brothers already owned thirty-five to forty neighborhood theaters and were building the glamorous Ambassador Theater in downtown St. Louis.

A movie house chain had been the American dream for George Skouras and his brothers, Charles and Spyros, the sons of a Greek sheepherder. Charles had emigrated first and worked as a busboy at the Jefferson Hotel. He saved his money to help his brothers emigrate. The three brothers were working as bartenders in 1914 when they bought an eight-hundred-seat nickelodeon at 1420 Market Street, now the site of the Peabody Opera House. Charles was the manager, Spyros sold tickets and swept the floors, and George collected the tickets. They invested their profits by buying other theaters.

Spyros Skouras became the chairman of the board of Twentieth Century Fox Film Corporation. George Skouras was chairman of the board of United Artists Theater Circuit Inc. at the time of his death in 1964.

The facade of the old movie house, minus the marquis and ticket booth, disguises a Mediterranean-style home and an art gallery. (Photo by Dylan Callahan)

Though the brothers lost their fortune in 1930, they quickly rebuilt it. Within two years, they were managing theaters from New York to Los Angeles.

Meanwhile, the Columbia movie house operated into the 1970s, when it was renovated as a racquet club. After a fire badly damaged the old movie house, it sat vacant for years. In 1987, artist and architect Frank K. Schwaiger renovated the movie house, turning it into a Mediterranean-style home with a heated pool in its open atrium. Gallery space in the complex serves as the Columbia Foundation for the Visual Arts.

THIS USED TO BE: A Greek American's Moving Picture Show

NOW IT'S: Private Residence on The Hill and the Columbia Foundation for the Visual Arts

LOCATION: 5329–33 Columbia

The Nation's Finest Victorian Park—Tower Grove Park

Fanciful gazebos, statuary, and wandering roadways punctuate the romantic nineteenth-century landscape of Tower Grove Park. The park's thousands of shade trees—including Osage orange trees with their baseball-sized fruit, towering bald cypresses, and exotic gingkoes with their fan-shaped leaves—shade its 289 acres. This urban park in South St. Louis is recognized as the finest example of a Victorian park in the entire nation. The delightful landscape almost disguises the park's sports fields, wading pool, and courts, which have enriched the lives of generations of young St. Louisans.

When nineteenth-century philanthropist Henry Shaw was guiding the planting and design of this park, his gift to St. Louisans, it was on the outskirts of the city. By the turn of the century, the eastern border of the park was evolving as the cultural spine of the German community, and a colony of Italian Americans was taking root on the high ground west of the park. That hardworking colony would grow into St. Louis' famous Italian neighborhood, The Hill. Two Italian American working-class families settled on Elizabeth Avenue on The Hill, the Garagiola family and the Berra family.

Stone and cast-iron gateway leading into Victorian-style Tower Grove Park. (Photo by Mark Scott Abeln)

St. Louis Cardinals catcher and later network sports announcer, Joe Garagiola (1926–2016), remembered Tower Grove Park as the place where he and his childhood friend and neighbor, Yogi Berra (1925–2015), played baseball. Berra would grow up to be a Hall of Famer and manager of the New York Yankees.

Garagiola described an incident in Tower Grove Park to explain that Yogi Berra was an athlete with talents in many sports.

"On this day we were playing on one end of the field, and the South West [Southwest] High School football team was working out at the other end. Well, a football got loose and came to our end and Yogi picked it up and kicked it back—a tremendous kick. He was wearing sneakers, and he must have kicked that football fifty yards. So the coach came over and wanted to know who kicked the ball. We told him it was Yogi. Right there, the coach asked him to come to South West High to play football.

"Yogi said he couldn't because he had to go to work. But the coach was persistent. 'Just come to school three days a week,' he said."

High school, however, was a luxury that Yogi Berra could not afford. Like so many children who grew up on The Hill, he went to work after graduating grade school because he needed to help with his family's bills.

THIS USED TO BE: The Ball Field for Future Italian American Big Leaguers

NOW IT'S: The Nation's Finest Victorian Park—Tower Grove Park

LOCATION: South St. Louis

87

A Lindenwood Neighborhood Cottage

A picturesque red-brick cottage at 6529 Mardel, with its gabled roof and stone trim, possesses the charm of its nearby houses and surrounding Lindenwood neighborhood in South City. Its history, however, sets it apart. The St. Louis city directory of 1947–48 carried this simple listing for the address: "Musial, Stanley (Lillian) baseball player Cardinals h6529 Mardell av." In front of its postage stamp–sized front yard, "Stanley The 'Man' Musial Lived Here 1948–1953" is painted into the concrete work of the curb.

The well-crafted cottage, with only a thousand square feet, must have seemed like a palace to the Musials. The son of a Polish immigrant who worked loading bales of wire onto freight cars, Stan Musial knew tough times. He recalled that his mother made baseballs for him "out of a little bit of this and that," including bits of yarn and tape. He worked various jobs to help with his family's bills, but his dream was to be a baseball player. At age seventeen he signed a contract with the Cardinals for $65 per month.

Stan Musial married his hometown sweetheart, Lillian Susan Labash (both were from the steel town of Donora, Pennsylvania). From the little South St. Louis cottage on Mardel, the Musials moved to 5447 Childress Avenue in the new St. Louis Hills Estates, a suburban-style development in South City. Then the Musials moved to a spacious new home nearby on Westway.

THIS USED TO BE: The Home of Stan Musial

NOW IT'S: A Lindenwood Neighborhood Cottage

LOCATION: 6529 Mardel Avenue

The Musial cottage in the Lindenwood neighborhood. (Photo by Dylan Weber Callahan)

A Northampton Neighborhood Hansel and Gretel Cottage

There is an aura about the home built in 1942 at the corner of Potomac Street and Sulphur Avenue. It looks like a house out of a fairy tale, with its steeply pitched roof and plentiful trim—a modern, streamlined version of the Hansel and Gretel–style houses so common in its Northampton neighborhood of South City. It is one of three similar houses constructed simultaneously by the same builder on the same block, each costing $4,500 to build.

What gives this particular house distinction is that it was once home to the Red Schoendienst family. The ballplayer from Germantown, Illinois, Albert "Red" Schoendienst married Mary Eileen O'Reilly in 1951. He had met Mary on the Grand Avenue streetcar. After they married, they lived in this cottage at 5800 Potomac.

Baby Boomers growing up on the same block that Cardinal Red Schoendienst lived on enjoyed a certain prestige. Even families who moved onto the block years later still gloried in the aura of Red Schoendienst's connection to their environs.

Discussing his career, Schoendienst stated, "The luckiest break for me was when I became Stan Musial's roommate." By 1958, the Schoendienst family were also neighbors of the Musial family. They had moved from the Potomac Street streamlined Hansel and Gretel house to the small ranch house at 6036 Highfield Road in St. Louis Hills Estates. Their new home was around the bend from the Musials' home on Westway. Like the Musial family, the Schoendienst family belonged to the new St. Raphael the Archangel Parish.

An outstanding second baseman, Schoendienst went on to manage the Cardinals. The Hall of Famer twice piloted the Cardinals to the World Series.

The home of Red and Mary Schoendienst in their Northampton neighborhood. (Photo by Dylan Weber Callahan)

THIS USED TO BE: The Red Schoendienst Home

NOW IT'S: A Northampton Neighborhood Hansel and Gretel Cottage

LOCATION: 5800 Potomac Street

89

St. Louis Hills Estates

Urban neighborhoods with grids of streets and blocks filled most of the city of St. Louis when developer Cyrus Crane Willmore began transforming the rolling landscape south of Francis Park into the new-style St. Louis Hills Estates. Willmore platted St. Louis Hills Estates No. 2 for development in 1945. It featured wandering roadways with rolling curbs and irregular-shaped lots planted with shade trees. The sprawling one-story houses had attached garages. This suburban-style development with cul-de-sacs and ranch houses would soon be home to two St. Louis Cardinals Hall of Famers.

A permit was issued to build a one-story brick home at 6451 Westway Road in St. Louis Hills Estates No. 2 in June 1955. Its estimated cost of construction was a then whopping $30,000. When the house was completed, Cardinals baseball player Stan Musial and his family moved into the ranch house from their nearby home at 5447 Childress Avenue. Almost immediately, Musial was issued a permit to construct an addition to the sprawling new home.

The school cafeteria is in the basement of St. Raphael the Archangel Parish School. (Photo by Nini Harris)

With 2,683 square feet, it was double the size of their home on Childress. Their almost childlike joy in their success endeared the Musials to a generation who, like them, understood the hardships of the Great Depression and World War II.

A regular meeting of the St. Raphael Parish Men's Club featured Stan Musial, Red Schoendienst, Joe Garagiola, and Bob Burns discussing the upcoming baseball season. The meeting was held in the current school cafeteria of St. Raphael the Archangel Parish at 6000 Jamieson Avenue.

A photo of Stan Musial in his batting stance at Sportsman's Park, ca. 1950. (Courtesy of the Missouri Historical Society)

The building permit issued to Stan Musial to build an addition onto his new home in St. Louis Hills Estates.

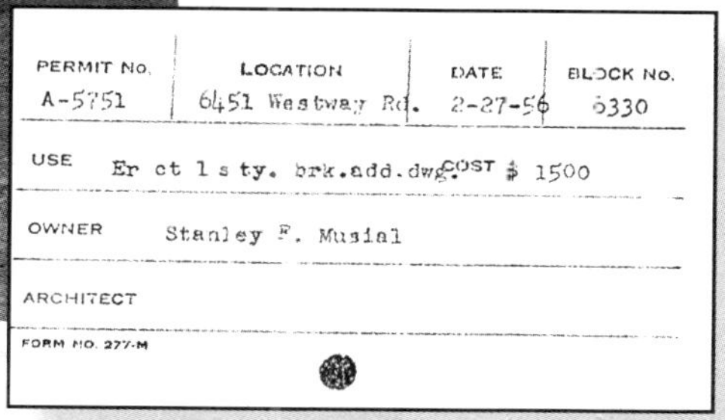

PERMIT NO.	LOCATION	DATE	BLOCK NO.
A-5751	6451 Westway Rd.	2-27-56	6330

USE Er ct 1 s ty. brk.add.dwg. COST $ 1500

OWNER Stanley F. Musial

ARCHITECT

FORM NO. 277-M

The Musial family were members of the new St. Raphael the Archangel Parish. At the same time, the parish roster also included the Red Schoendienst family, *Globe-Democrat* sportswriter Bob Burns, and big-league catcher Joe Garagiola.

THIS USED TO BE: The Hall of Famers' Neighborhood

NOW IT'S: St. Louis Hills Estates

LOCATION: South St. Louis

Jefferson Barracks Park

A tent city that was home to thousands of young soldiers once covered the rolling lawns of Jefferson Barracks Park. The parkland perched above the Mississippi River was part of the military post established in 1826 that by the 1840s became the largest military post in the United States. Two hundred Civil War generals, from both the Union and Confederate armies, at one time served at the South County army post. In World War I, nearly a quarter of a million young men were inducted into or discharged from the US Army at Jefferson Barracks.

As the nation ramped up to face the Axis in World War II, Jefferson Barracks became home to the Army Air Corps training schools. The capacity of the barracks was rapidly expanding due to the construction of frame and tent barracks. In September 1941, workers with the Depression-era employment program, the Works Progress Administration (WPA), constructed 1,700 tent frames for a new camp area in the barracks. It was reported that this new area would accommodate eight thousand more men.

Since Jefferson Barracks also served as an induction center, World War II began for many St. Louis boys with a streetcar ride on the tracks that led right into Jefferson Barracks. Its 1,702 acres were crowded with two-story frame barracks and hundreds of large tents, heated by stoves, lining the dirt paths of the tent cities.

When the war finally ended, the War Department declared Jefferson Barracks surplus. Eventually, 425 acres of the historic barracks became Jefferson Barracks Park. Where young men had lived in tents and trained for war, today children play, folks enjoy the awe-inspiring views of the Mississippi, and visitors tour historic displays in stone-walled powder magazines from the 1850s.

In August 1940, the Sixth Infantry was withdrawn from Jefferson Barracks, ending its role as an infantry training post. By September, the barracks had been designated as the Army Air Corps training site.

A postcard showing some of Jefferson Barrack's World War II–era tent cities. As the war continued, cabin-like prefab structures called "hutments" gradually replaced many of the tents. (Postcard from a private collection)

THIS USED TO BE: A Tent City

NOW IT'S: Jefferson Barracks Park

LOCATION: South St. Louis County

ENDNOTES

[1]"Spanish Pavilion Described as 'the Jewel of the Fair.'" *St. Louis Post-Dispatch*, October 28, 1965.

[2]Cervantes, A. J. *Mr. Mayor* (Los Angeles: Nash Publishing, 1974), 124.

[3]Dreiser, Theodore, *A Book about Myself*, 110.

[4]Ibid., 174.

[5]Historic postcard. Private Collection.

[6]"Pendennis Club Building Sold," *St. Louis Globe-Democrat*, May 9, 1937.

[7]Coghlan, Ralph, "St. Louis Letter." *St. Louis Post-Dispatch*, December 14, 1949.

[8]*St. Louis Globe-Democrat*, October 2, 1953. Clipping files, St. Louis Public Library.

[9]*St. Louis Post-Dispatch*, August 29, 1954. Clipping files, St. Louis Public Library.

[10]Lindbergh, Charles A., *The Spirit of St. Louis* (New York: Charles Scribner's Sons, 1953), 21.

[11]Ibid., 21.

[12]Williams, Tennessee. *Memoirs* (New York: Bantam Books, 1976), 17.

[13] This was a statement made by Neighborhood Marketing Services when that organization featured a unit in Dorris Lofts as its "House of the Month." *St. Louis Globe Democrat*, September 6–7, 1986. "September House of Month is rehabbed, upscale residence," the statement said.

[14]"Singing Sam." *The Saturday Evening Post*, February 22, 1947.

[15]1941 St. Louis Parks and Recreation Department Annual Report

[16]1942 St. Louis Parks and Recreation Department Annual Report, p. 2.

[17]"$20,000 Chicken Farm Is Bought for L. Busch Faust." *St. Louis Post-Dispatch*, July 2, 1917.

[18]"Gute Erinnerungen von West County." *Summit* (Maryville College, St. Louis), Vol. 3, No. 6 (April 1980).

[19]Fund-raising brochure published in the spring of 1896 to assist with rebuilding Lafayette Park Presbyterian Church and the Soulard Market Mission. Found in the collections of Tyler Place Presbyterian Church.

[20]"Mr. Softie," *St. Louis Post-Dispatch*, November 2, 2004.

[21]Ibid.

[22]Personal memoirs by Carolyn Hackman of her childhood at 39th Street and Russell Boulevard. Prepared by Hackman for her extended family members. Found in the archives of Tyler Place Presbyterian Church in the Shaw neighborhood.

SOURCES

Jefferson National Expansion Memorial
Dreiser, Theodore. *A Book about Myself* (New York: Horace Liveright, 1922), 206.

MetroLink Tunnel
Hyde, William, and Howard L. Conard, eds. *Encyclopedia of the History of St. Louis* (New York, Louisville, St. Louis: The Southern History Company, 1899). Vollmar, Joseph E. *James B. Eads and the Great St. Louis Bridge* (St. Louis: The Engineers' Club of St. Louis, 1974). Joseph E. Vollmar Jr. was president of the Engineers' Club from 1973 to 1974. The club is located at 4359 Lindell Boulevard.

Streets of Laclede's Landing
Plat of St. Louis with All the Houses on March 10, 1804. From the original prepared by Frederick Billon, traced by Norbury Wayman. This map shows each building and its method of construction.

Raeder Place
Plat of St. Louis with All the Houses on March 10, 1804. From the original prepared by Frederick Billon, traced by Norbury Wayman. "Architectural Map of Laclede's Landing," Saint Louis Chapter, American Institute of Architects, 1978. Raeder Place Dedication program, Thursday, April 30, 1998.

William A. Kerr Foundation
North Riverfront Industrial Historic District, National Register of Historic Places registration form, by Lynn Josse, 2002. "An End to a Tale of Glory and Decline," *St. Louis Globe-Democrat*, April 5, 1976.

Hilton at the Ballpark
"The Spanish Pavilion, 'Jewel' of the New York World's Fair Coveted by Mayor Cervantes," *St. Louis Post-Dispatch* Pictures section, November 7, 1965. McCue, George. *The Building Art in St. Louis: Two Centuries*, 3rd ed. (St. Louis: The St. Louis Chapter of the American Institute of Architects Foundation, Knight Publishing Co., 1981).

Spire Energy Headquarters
St. Louis Post-Dispatch, September 23, 1902. *St. Louis Post-Dispatch*, January 28, 1894. "St. Louis Chinatown Loses Old Glamor," *St. Louis Post-Dispatch*, July 18, 1923. Ling, Huping. *Chinese St. Louis: From Enclave to Cultural Community* (Philadelphia: Temple University Press, 2004).

Walnut Street at 7th Street
Orear, G. W. *Commercial and Architectural St. Louis* (Jones & Orear, Publishers, 1888). *St. Louis Globe-Democrat*, April 9, 1961. Yeatman, Ted P. *Frank and Jesse James: The Story behind the Legend* (Nashville: Cumberland House, 2000).

Drury Inn & Suites Convention Center
Taylor, Philip. A *Brief History of the Public Markets and Private Markets Referred to as Public Markets in the City of St. Louis Missouri* (City of St. Louis, January 1961). Private Collection. Taylor was the city's market master.

Bailey's Range and Apartments
Park, David G., Jr. *Good Connections: A Century of Service by the Men & Women of Southwestern Bell* (Southwestern Bell Telephone Company, 1984).

Market Street from 18th to 20th Streets
"Birth, Deeds and Death of the "Bottoms" Gang," *St. Louis Post-Dispatch*, March 14, 1909. Waugh, Daniel, *Egan's Rats: The Untold Story of the Prohibition-Era Gang That Ruled St. Louis* (Nashville: Cumberland House, 2007).

2020 Washington Condominiums
Know St. Louis Weekly, March, 11, 1928. "New Emerson Building Will Cost $600,000," *St. Louis Post-Dispatch*, December 17, 1919."

Washington Avenue Loft District
Purdy, Harry L. *An Historical Analysis of the Economic Growth of St. Louis, 1840–1945.* Oestreich, Kenneth D. *Historic St. Louis: An Architectural Survey of the Central Business District* (Prepared for the City of St. Louis Community Development Agency, 1977).

Ely Walker Lofts
Hyde, William, and Howard L. Conard, eds. *Encyclopedia of the History of St. Louis* (New York, Louisville, St. Louis: The Southern History Company, 1899). *St. Louis Globe-Democrat*, May 25, 1965.

Schlafly Tap Room
Schlafly, Tom. "A St. Louis Story." 2016. Schlafly is chairman of the board of the Saint Louis Brewery LLC. Lambert-Deacon-Hull Printing Company Building/Swift Printing Company Building, National Register of Historic Places nomination form, by the Landmarks Association of St. Louis, 1980. Marquis, Albert Nelson, ed. *The Book of St. Louisans, A Biographical Dictionary of the Leading Living Men of the City of St. Louis and Vicinity,* 2nd ed. (Chicago: A. N. Marquis and Company, 1912).

Saint Louis University's Campus East of Grand
Rombauer, Robert Julius. *The Union Cause in St. Louis in 1861: An Historical Sketch* (St. Louis: Press of Nixon-Jones Printing Company, 1909). Sherman, William Tecumseh. *Memoirs of General William T. Sherman, by Himself*, Volume I (New York: D. Appleton and Company, 1891).

City House in Grand Center Arts District
St. Louis city directories. *Grand Center Inc.: Celebrating 30 Years of the Arts and Civic Leadership* (St. Louis: Grand Center Inc., 2011). Compton, Richard J., and Camille N. Dry. *Pictorial St. Louis, the Great Metropolis of the Mississippi Valley: A Topographical Survey Drawn in Perspective, A. D. 1875* (St. Louis: Compton & Co., 1876).

Saint Louis University's Office of Admissions
"Bought: Women's Club Planned," *St. Louis Post-Dispatch*, April 23, 1939. "Queen's Daughters' Home to Celebrate Golden Jubilee," *St. Louis Globe-Democrat*, September 21, 1947. "Queen's Daughters' Home Evangeline Residence to Close," *St. Louis Post-Dispatch*, May 24, 1972.

Saint Louis University Museum of Art
Ayotte, Diane Boucher. "A Guide to Private Organizations, Clubs and Societies, ca. 1820–1930." Missouri Historical Society, St. Louis, 1990.

The House at 4232 McPherson Avenue
Seyersted, Per E. "Kate Chopin: An Important St. Louis Writer Reconsidered." *Bulletin of the Missouri Historical Society*, Volume XIX (January 1963), pages 89–114. Seyersted, Per E., *Kate Chopin: A Critical Biography* (Oslo, Norway: Universitesforlaget; Baton Rouge: Louisiana State University Press, 1969).

Pulitzer Arts Foundation Offices
Ayotte, Diane Boucher. "A Guide to Private Organizations, Clubs and Societies, ca. 1820–1930." Missouri Historical Society, St. Louis, 1990. "Pendennis Club Building Sold," *St. Louis Globe-Democrat*, May 9, 1937.

Vacant Lot at 4460 Delmar Boulevard

Obituary of Jordan W. Chambers, *St. Louis Post-Dispatch*, August 11, 1962. Obituary of Jordan W. Chambers, *St. Louis Globe-Democrat*, August 11, 1962. *St. Louis Post-Dispatch,* untitled clipping in St. Louis Public Library catalogue file, November 6, 1970.

An Contemporary Urban Forest

St. Louis Globe-Democrat, October 2, 1953. *St. Louis Post-Dispatch*, August 29, 1954. Primm, James Neal. *Lion of the Valley: St. Louis, Missouri, 1764–1980.* Reprint. (St. Louis: Missouri Historical Society Press, 1998).

An Urban Forest in the Mid-Ninteenth Century

Faherty, William B. *St. Louis Irish: An Unmatched Celtic Community* (St. Louis: Missouri Historical Society Press, 2001). "Memories of Historic Locality Gleaned from the Last King of Kerry Patch," *St. Louis Globe-Democrat*, December 31, 1905.

The Last Landmark of Kerry Patch

City of St. Louis building permits. "Jack Sheahan, Former King of Kerry Patch Here, Dies at 83," *St. Louis Star-Times*, November 15, 1935. "John J. Sheahan Dies at 83 after Operation," *St. Louis Post-Dispatch*, January 15, 1935. "Memories of Historic Locality Gleaned from the Last King of Kerry Patch," *St. Louis Globe-Democrat*, December 31, 1905.

George B. Vashon African American Museum

St. Louis Post-Dispatch obituary of James Meagher, November 16, 1899.

A Polish Fraternal Hall

Interviews conducted in 2006 and 2007 with longtime members of the Polish Falcons. Papers, programs, and ephemera saved by the Falcons. Hyde, William, and Howard L. Conard, eds. *Encyclopedia of the History of St. Louis* (New York, Louisville, St. Louis: The Southern History Company, 1899).

A Storage Building

Annual reports of the St. Louis Parks and Recreation Department. *Municipal Journal and Engineer* (New York) Volume XXX, No. 15, April 12, 1911. Wells, Rolla. *Episodes of My Life* (St. Louis: McCarthy, 1933).

Senior Apartments in the Ville Neighborhood

"Inspiration of the Negro Hospital Fight," *St. Louis Post-Dispatch*, February 23, 1937. "Negroes Moved into New Hospital, Old City Institution Abandoned," *St. Louis Star-Times*, June 1, 1937. "World's Finest Negro Hospital Dedicated," *St. Louis Globe-Democrat*, February 23, 1937.

Fort Belle Fontaine Park

Smith, Jeffrey E., ed. *Seeking a Newer World: The Fort Osage Journals and Letters of George Sibley, 1808–1811* (St. Charles: Lindenwood University Press, 2003). Wilson, Robert. "History of Fort Bellefontaine," January 7, 1982. Carondelet Historical Society Collections.

Bellefontaine Road

History of Old Roads, Pioneer Settlers and Early Communities of St. Louis County, Watchman Advocate, ca. 1940. *Pitzman's New Atlas of the City and County of Saint Louis, Missouri* (Philadelphia: A. B. Holcombe & Co., 1878).

St. Louis Lambert International Airport

Interviews with Benny and Billie Von Baudissin conducted in 1976. Louise Helen Harris, mother of the author, repeatedly described her ride in an open-cockpit plane taking off from Lambert Field.

Urshan College
Killoren, John J. *Jesuit Roots and Pioneer Heroes of the Middle West* (Florissant, Mo.: St. Stanislaus Jesuit Historical Museum, ca. 1988). Drawings and photos of the seminary in the collections of the Missouri Province Archives. Rothensteiner, Rev. John. *History of the Archdiocese of St. Louis* (St. Louis: Press of Blackwell Wielandy Co., 1928).

2 Hortense Place
"A. B. Lambert Dies in Sleep; Burial Tomorrow," *St. Louis Globe-Democrat*, November 13, 1946. Proof for *The Blue Book of Aviation*, Los Angeles, California, St. Louis Public Library. "St. Louis Aviation Pioneers, Albert Bond Lambert," *Missouri Historical Society Bulletin* Winter 1998, 7.

Dorris Loft Condominiums
The National Register of Historic Places nomination form for the building submitted in 1985 and prepared by Carolyn H. Toft and Cynthia Longwisch of the Landmarks Association of St. Louis Inc. St. Louis' Early Auto Makers: From Carriages to Cars, *St. Louis Commerce*, October 1981.

Evangeline's Bistro
Street commissioner's certificates. St. Louis city directories. "Baseball World to Pay Tribute to Sam Breadon," *St. Louis Globe-Democrat,* January 13, 1948. "Horatio Alger Touch to Story of Sam Breadon," *St. Louis Post-Dispatch,* May 11, 1949. "Sam Breadon Dies at 72, Ex-owner of Cardinals; No Public Funeral," *St. Louis Post-Dispatch*, May 11, 1949. Waters, Paul, "By the Mississippi" (column), *St. Louis Times,* May 14, 1947. Keener, Sid, "Cards and Browns" (column), *St. Louis Times,* June 11, 1947.

Forest Park (The Southeastern Corner)
Annual reports of the St. Louis Parks and Recreation Department.

Missouri Historical Society Library and Research Center
Compton, Richard J., and Camille N. Dry. *Pictorial St. Louis, the Great Metropolis of the Mississippi Valley: A Topographical Survey Drawn in Perspective, A. D. 1875* (St. Louis: Compton & Co., 1876). Ehrlich, Walter E. *Zion in the Valley: The Jewish Community of St. Louis; Volume II, the Twentieth Century* (Columbia: University of Missouri Press, 1997). Stiritz, Mary M. *St. Louis: Historic Churches & Synagogues* (St. Louis: St. Louis Public Library and Landmarks Association of St. Louis Inc., 1995). Wofford, Theodore, "From Temple to Library: The Architect's Point of View," *Focus*, January/February 1992.

A Clayton Neighborhood
Dickson, Terry. *Clayton: A History* (Clayton, Mo.: City of Clayton, 1976).

Leon R. Strauss Center of the Community Music School
"Mary Plant Faust, 95; Civic Leader and Philanthropist," *St. Louis Post-Dispatch*, May 5, 1996. Terry, Elizabeth. *Oysters to Angus: Three Generations of the St. Louis Faust Family* (St. Louis: Bluebird Publishing, 2014).

Frontenac Hilton Hotel
Interview with David Block, March 20, 2017. Advertising on promotional postcards.

Maryville Centre Corporate Park
"40-Year-Old Log Cabin Moving to New Address in 19th Century Village," *St. Louis Globe-Democrat*, July 10, 1986. "Historic Case of Cabin Fever," *St. Louis Post-Dispatch*, July 25, 1986. "Part 2 of Maryville Office Complex Takes Root," undated *St. Louis Post-Dispatch* newspaper clipping in Maryville University Archives.

Park Avenue Plaza
Compton, Richard J., and Camille N. Dry. *Pictorial St. Louis, the Great Metropolis of the Mississippi Valley: A Topographical Survey Drawn in Perspective, A. D. 1875* (St. Louis: Compton & Co., 1876). Prost, Charlene, "From Junkyard to Jewel," *St. Louis Post-Dispatch*,

September 12, 2004. Rice, Patricia, "New Plaza Is Latest Addition to '30-Year Project' of Revival at Lafayette Square," *St. Louis Post-Dispatch*, September 16, 2004.

A Lafayette Square Victorian Town House
Orear, G. W. *Commercial and Architectural St. Louis* (Jones & Orear, Publishers, 1888). The author visited the house during the early stages of its renovation in 1976.

Abbey on the Park Condominiums
Ranken, Robert. "Historical Sketch of the Church," published March 31, 1903. Ranken was president of the church's board of trustees.

Turnverein Condominiums
"City Equity's Turnverein Condominiums," *Saint Louis Rehabber*, October 1981. *St. Louis Globe-Democrat Sunday Magazine*, February 26, 1961.

St. John's Lofts
Harris, NiNi. *Bohemian Hill: An American Experience* (St. Louis: St. John Nepomuk Parish, 2004). *Souvenir of Diamond Jubilee, St. John Nepomuk Parish, Sunday, Nov. 24, to Thursday, Nov. 28, 1929* (St. Louis: Tiskem "Hlasu," 1929).

Obata, a Creative Communications Firm
Fund-raising brochure published in the spring of 1896 to assist with rebuilding Lafayette Park Presbyterian Church and the Soulard Market Mission. Found in the collections of Tyler Place Presbyterian Church. Ranken, Robert. *Historical Sketch of the Church, Lafayette Park Presbyterian Church*, undated. Found in the collections of Tyler Place Presbyterian Church. "Two Historic Presbyterian Churches to Merge," *The Carondelet Presbyterian*, ca. 1957. Collections of Carondelet Historical Society.

Soulard Preservation Hall
Sheldon, Walter L. "The Wage Earners' Self-Culture Clubs of St. Louis: A Sketch of Their History." *Ethical Addresses*, Series VII, Nos. 3–4, March–April 1900.

Barlog-Kuszaj-Zero American Legion Post
Records of Our Lady of Czestochowa Parish, St. Louis Archdiocesan Archives. Interviews with Joseph Rudawski in 2006. Lange, Dena, and Merlin M. Ames. *St. Louis: Child of the River, Parent of the West* (St. Louis: Webster Publishing Company, 1939). Park, David G., Jr. *Good Connections: A Century of Service by the Men & Women of Southwestern Bell* (St. Louis: Southwestern Bell Telephone Company, 1984).

Big Daddy's Bar and Grill
Compton, Richard J., and Camille N. Dry. *Pictorial St. Louis, the Great Metropolis of the Mississippi Valley: A Topographical Survey Drawn in Perspective, A. D. 1875* (St. Louis: Compton & Co., 1876). Kennedy's Sectional Map of St. Louis, 1859. Traced by Norbury Wayman. St. Louis Public Library. Rombauer, Robert J. *The Union Cause in St. Louis in 1861: An Historical Sketch* (St. Louis: Press of Nixon-Jones, 1909).

Benton Park
Annual Reports of the St. Louis Parks Department. Kargau, Ernst D. *St. Louis in Former Years: A Commemorative History of the German Element.* William G. Bek, trans. Don Heinrich Tolzmann, ed. (Columbia: University of Missouri Press, 1943). "St. Louis Area Cemeteries." Compiled by the Microfilm Department and History & Genealogy Department, St. Louis Public Library, 2005. Lange, Dena, and Merlin M. Ames. *St. Louis: Child of the River, Parent of the West* (St. Louis: Webster Publishing Company, 1939).

Senate Square
Compton, Richard J., and Camille N. Dry. *Pictorial St. Louis, the Great Metropolis of the Mississippi Valley: A Topographical Survey Drawn in Perspective, A. D. 1875* (St. Louis:

Compton & Co., 1876). "Fortifications of Civil War Period." In *Encyclopedia of the History of St. Louis,* edited by William Hyde and Howard L. Conard (New York, Louisville, St. Louis: The Southern History Company, 1899), 814–816.

The Historic Benton Park Neighborhood
Interview with Charles Marvin, retired St. Louis Metropolitan Police officer, December 2016.

Victorian Storefront at 1976–82 Arsenal
Auble, John, Jr., "Brother of Ray Found Hiding Himself Here," *St. Louis Globe-Democrat,* May 22, 1968. "Authorities Here Remember Ray as Drifter, Typical Hoodlum," *St. Louis Post-Dispatch,* April 20, 1968. "Brothers of Ray Postpone Their Reunion in Memphis," *St. Louis Globe-Democrat,* July 23, 1968.

STL Style House
Interview with Joseph and Clara Venverloh's granddaughter, Rosemary Aprill Crespi, in 1999.

Morgan Ford Business District
Woodcock, Lyle S. "The St. Louis Heritage of Charles Marion Russell," *Gateway Heritage,* Vol. 2, No. 4 (Spring 1982).

Moth Repellent and Urinal Cake Manufactory
Scharf, J. Thomas. *History of St. Louis City and County* (Philadelphia: Louis H. Everts & Co., 1883). Orear, G. W. *Commercial and Architectural St. Louis* (Jones & Orear, Publishers, 1888). Hyde, William, and Howard L. Conard, eds. *Encyclopedia of the History of St. Louis* (New York, Louisville, St. Louis: The Southern History Company, 1899). Harris, NiNi. *Unyielding Spirit: The History of the Polish People of St. Louis* (St. Louis: St. Stanislaus Kostka Parish, 2007).

An Apartment Complex
Who's Who in North St. Louis (St. Louis: North St. Louis Business Men's Association, 1925).

Beck Avenue in South St. Louis
Boyer, Mary Joan. *The Old Gravois Coal Diggings* (Festus, Mo.: Tri-City Independent Printer 1952). *Pitzman's New Atlas of the City and County of Saint Louis, Missouri* (Philadelphia: A. B. Holcombe & Co., 1878).

U-Haul
"South City National Candy Building to Become U-Haul Storage Facility," Nextstl.com, September 22, 2015.

A Dutchtown Neighborhood
Eike photo collection, Carondelet Historical Society. Sanborn fire insurance map, December 1916. *St. Pius V Parish, St. Louis, Missouri, 1905–1980* (St. Louis, 1980).

A Mount Pleasant Neighborhood
"Carondelet Priest Sells Building Lots," *Carondelet News,* September 10, 1904. *Silver Jubilee of the St. Hedwig Parish, 1904–1929.*

Pasta Plant and Barge Line
Map of Proposed Navy Yard in Carondelet, St. Louis Co., Mo. (Philadelphia: Bowen & Co. lithographers, 1864), Carondelet Historical Society. Scharf, J. Thomas. *History of St. Louis City and County* (Philadelphia: Louis H. Everts & Co., 1883).

Water Fountain in the Ivory Triangle
Writings of Ernest E. Winkelmann, grandson of Daniel Paule. *Carondelet Historical Society Newsletter,* Vol. 5, No. 1 (March 1973).

Carondelet Historical Society
"Another Cook's Supermarket Opens." Clipping from unidentified paper, October 12, 1960,

on file in the Carondelet Historical Society's archives. "Roy L. Tarter," *Naborhood Link News*, January 29, 1947. "Site of First Kindergarten Class in U.S. May Be Sold," *St. Louis Post-Dispatch*, September 14, 1945. Souvenir booklet for the grand opening of LaVerne Park on Saturday, August 16, 1947. "Supermarket Will Occupy Site of Susan Blow's Kindergarten," *St. Louis Post-Dispatch*, October 4, 1959.

Boulevard Heights Neighborhood
The Knackstedt Family Album, Carondelet Historical Society. St. Louis Public Library Report of 1911–12 in the St. Louis Public Library collections.

Private Residence on the Hill and the Columbia Foundation for the Visual Arts
Advertisement in 1927 St. Louis city directory, p. 315. Obituary of George Skouras, *St. Louis Post-Dispatch*, March 17, 1964.

The Nation's Finest Victorian Park—Tower Grove Park
Pepe, Phil. *The Wit and Wisdom of Yogi Berra* (New York: An Associated Features Book Hawthorn Books, Inc., 1974).

A Northampton Neighborhood Hansel and Gretel Cottage
Albert "Red" Schoendienst induction speech to the Baseball Hall of Fame, 1989. Frederick Hodes, St. Raphael the Archangel Parish History Committee.

Jefferson Barracks Park
Interview at Jefferson Barracks with Winfred "Wimpy" Kenner on August 4, 2017. Interview with Rose Ann Klingl Fanz on March 3, 1995. "WPA Constructing 1700 Tent Frames at the Barracks," *Watchman Advocate*, September 19, 1941. "Jefferson Barracks—Preparing Men for Air Corps Technical Schools," June 18, 1941, St. Louis Public Library clipping files.

OTHER SOURCES

While specific articles, interviews, books, and documents have been listed as sources for individual chapters, other sources of information were used to research almost every individual site or property. The directories used include *Gould's Blue Book for the City of St. Louis* (a directory of financially and socially prominent citizens), *Gould's Commercial Register of the City of St. Louis*, *Gould's St. Louis Red-Blue Book*, *Gould's St. Louis Directory*, and *Polk's St. Louis City Directory*.

Building permits maintained by the Comptroller's Office of the City of St. Louis were a source of information for many of the buildings.

For some of the properties, the ownership was traced through the decades using the records maintained in the Assessor's Office of the City of St. Louis.

Street numbering certificates, maintained by St. Louis Public Library Special Collections, were used to date buildings.

Information concerning the architects and builders of city properties was researched using the *St. Louis Daily Record*, the legal newspaper.

US census records provided a wealth of information.

ACKNOWLEDGMENTS

The following individuals assisted with locating information for this book:

St. Louis Public Library staff members Amanda Bahr-Evola, Third Floor manager; Adele Heagney and Kirwin Roach in the St. Louis Room; Kristina Impastato and Renee Jones in Special Collections; Cynthia Millar, Thomas Pearson, and Kyle Criner in the Genealogy Room; and Jason Sutterfield in the Business, Government & Law Room.

Missouri Historical Society staff member Jaime Bourassa.

Carondelet Historical Society volunteers Dave Bouchein, Bob Fox, Jerry Martin, and Mary Ann Simon.

Maryville University Library archivist Emma Prince.

Esley Hamilton, historian with the St. Louis County Historic Buildings Commission.

Jefferson Barracks Park volunteer Don Roberts.

St. Raphael the Archangel Parish History Committee member Frederick Hodes.

IBEW Local 1 historian John Kahrhoff.

Pius the XII Library, Saint Louis University, outreach coordinator John Waide.

Special thanks to Kathy Kasznel, Amanda McMichael, Emma Prince, and Roman Kordal, without whom this book would not have been possible.

INDEX